Go thou and do likewise

GIVING THEM HELL

How a College
_____

Professor Organized
_____

and Led a Successful
_____

Statewide Union

SIDNEY LIPSHIRES

Acknowledgements

The subtitle of this book is, "How a College Professor Organized and Led a Successful Statewide Union." However, when one reads the book, it soon becomes apparent that I was not the only person who had something to do with creating this union. Twelve different community college campuses joined together to form the Congress of Connecticut Community Colleges, and on each of these 12 campuses were many dedicated labor activists. Unionism was in the air, and had not this "college professor" been present, I believe that other determined people would have formed their own coalition. I could not possibly name here all the leaders and activists whose hard work built the success of the 4 C's, but they are the real heroes and heroines of this story.

Attorney Dan Livingston and former Connecticut Higher Education Commissioner Andrew G. De Rocco contributed some very cogent conceptual comments on early versions of this book. My daughter Lisa retyped all of my work—without my errors—and, more importantly, served as a tremendous editor. Any remaining errors, however, belong solely to me.

Table of Contents

Preface

THIS BOOK IS ABOUT A SUCCESSFUL UNION FOR CONNECTICUT community college faculty and professionals that I helped to organize and then led for 18 years. In these troubled times, when union membership has dropped, and unions in general have fallen in the national esteem, I think it is important to talk about examples of unions that actually achieved what their founders set out to do: protect the interests and rights of workers, and raise their members' economic standing. As you will see, bringing my union into being, and then defending its members' rights from many attacks, was not an easy proposition. In fact, the whole process could best be described as a struggle from beginning to end. However, when peoples' livelihoods and dignity are at stake, I believe that any amount of effort is worthwhile.

My interest in banding together to defend my own and others' rights began in Northampton, Massachusetts, the small college town where I grew up. In my junior year at Northampton High School, some other students and I organized a group called the Young Progressives, with the aim of instituting a number of school reforms. We published **The Hamp Lamp**, which may have been one of the first underground high school newspapers in the country, and we sent a list of our plans for reform to school and city officials. Like any good negotiators, we aimed high: among other things, we wanted a new high school, a school band, and a track team. We thought, at one point, that our high school principal was going to accede to our demands: he promised us that he would, in any case, if we called off a traditional day of high jinx and acting-up that we had been scheming to revive. We learned a bitter lesson, however, when the principal refused to deliver on his promises: always get it in writing.

My parents, too, had a strong influence on my later activism. My mother was a very intelligent and deeply religious woman who taught me to pay attention to the needs of those less fortunate than myself. My father was a successful businessman and civic leader, who was known for his honesty, thoroughness, and innovative thinking. I believe my parents were startled and displeased when I turned their exemplary qualities to good use in causes that were left of center, but I was always grateful for their model of socially responsible behavior.

As I describe in Chapter Three, my college experiences led me to join the Communist Party—a decision that at the time made a lot of sense, but that I later regretted as a mistake. I felt betrayed and bruised by the revelations of the 1950's that the Soviets had been perpetrating the violent suppression of democratic movements, but my commitment to bettering the lot of working people remained true. One of the reasons that I decided to teach in a community college system was that I felt I could make more of a difference there both for workers who had been undervalued and for students who had struggled to find an affordable education. The community college's mission of an accessible education for all was shared by the teachers and staff with whom I had the privilege to found a union. My hope is that the story of the challenges and successes we faced will inspire other people to take their own steps toward unity and empowerment.

GIVING THEM
HELL

CHAPTER

1

In the Beginning: Building Our Strength at Manchester

BEFORE THERE WAS A UNION, THERE WAS SOLIDARITY. IT WAS 1967, and I had been teaching history at Manchester Community College in Connecticut for a little over a year when we as a faculty launched our first large-scale labor action. I had observed that the teachers at Manchester were among the most active, labor-wise, in the state's twelve community colleges, but I had not expected that so many of us would be ready to jump into the fray. Perhaps I shouldn't have been surprised: our teachers had been heavily recruited from local high schools, where many had had broad experience with the two leading national teachers' unions, the National Education Association, and the American Federation of Teachers.

The issue that had our faculty up in arms was a proposal from our college's president that could affect our wage-earning abilities. In the high schools and in community colleges, wage scales depended in part on one's amount of previous experience, and also partly on one's level of education. A Ph.D. would provide the highest salary, but a doctorate was difficult for a teacher to obtain

1

because it required the writing of a lengthy dissertation. To be hired at a community college, teachers had to have, at a minimum, a Master's degree. The usefulness of a doctorate at either the high school or the community college level was questionable, especially since dissertations were often written on highly specialized topics. Writing a dissertation mainly demonstrated that a person could write a dissertation: it offered no proof that a person was qualified to teach.

To respond to the educational and professional needs of high school and community college teachers, some discussions had sprung up around the nation about the possibility of a new type of degree, the Doctor of Arts. A Doctor of Arts degree would have similar requirements to a Ph.D. or Ed.D., with the same coursework and written and oral exams, but would exclude the need for a dissertation. One person who liked this idea was Dr. Frederick Lowe, Jr., the president of Manchester Community College. He began to push for the creation of a Doctor of Arts degree for teachers at Connecticut community colleges, to be awarded by a committee made up only of college deans and presidents.

Though the faculty at Manchester was in favor of the concept of a Doctor of Arts degree, we were adamantly opposed to the practice of any degree being awarded by management personnel. The norm at universities across the land was for committees of faculty to award graduate degrees to students in their own academic departments. This practice was considered a right of faculty self-governance. If Fred Lowe's idea came to fruition, then this valued tradition would be overthrown. One of the dangers of allowing management personnel to decide on the awarding of graduate degrees was that faculty members could feel inhibited in the free expression of their ideas if they knew that someone with the power to promote or fire them was on their degree committee. In our view, this problem would be exacerbated by the fact that only three of the twelve community college presidents in the state could be relied on to make decisions that were in the best interests of the professional staff.

We knew that Dr. Lowe would be putting his idea to a vote at our next Professional Staff Meeting at Manchester, and we wanted to make sure that we had enough votes to roundly defeat his proposal. To that end, we drew up a petition in opposition to his plan, and asked all faculty members to sign it. This was our way of locking in the vote. A great majority of the teachers signed on. The day before the Professional Staff Meeting, we held a faculty caucus, attended by approximately forty-five teachers, in which we decided that we would use Robert's Rules of Order the next day to prevent debate over the issue. Through an overwhelming rejection of the proposal, we wanted to communicate our contempt for any idea that flew in the face of established practices of academic freedom and faculty governance.

Just before the Professional Staff Meeting the next day, I went up to Fred Lowe as a courtesy, and told him what we intended to do. "Go ahead," said Lowe, who was a big believer in free speech. The meeting started, and one of the faculty got up and made a motion to vote on our position. Then, a couple of teachers who had not attended the caucus the day before rose to speak in support of our ideas. As soon as they finished, another teacher "moved the previous question," which meant that we were closing down all debate, and bringing our petition to a vote. About 95% of those present voted "yes," in favor of our position. Among the "yes" votes were several deans, whom we had assumed would be in the President's camp.

This vote demonstrated solidarity in action, and was just the first in a number of similar actions at Manchester, all designed to show staff solidarity and the power to create a workable majority. A couple of years later, an internal dispute at Manchester led to the attempted firing of a division director and two others from the Continuing Education staff. A well-attended emergency meeting was called at my house, which led to the proposed firings being canceled. Good people not connected with any union movement were active in this effort, along with those who could have been described as ideologically in favor of unions. Over the next two years, some of the "solidarity people" from my campus were also active in a successful movement to add health and retirement benefits to the collective bargaining law for state employees. All of these actions of solidarity opened the door to the possibility of forming a union.

Manchester Community College was founded in 1963, three years before I began to work there as a teacher. During the early days of the college, there was growing discussion among the staff about the value of creating a faculty senate on our campus. Our plan was to include in this senate not only faculty, but also counselors, librarians, and some administrators, such as the Director of Admissions. Fred Lowe was generally in favor of the creation of such a body, but he did not like my suggestion that Bob Fenn, our Dean of Faculty, serve as its Chair. The standard practice at schools around the country was that the Dean of

Faculty also served as that college's Faculty Senate Chair. I had talked to Bob Fenn more than once about my proposal, and when I asked him why he thought Fred Lowe objected to his leadership, he answered, "He's afraid that, with the Dean of Faculty as Chair, the proposed senate would then pass resolutions." I couldn't help bursting into laughter. "Well," I said, "what's to stop us from passing resolutions in any event? We don't even need a faculty senate for that. There is a restaurant near the campus, and they encourage large groups to use their meeting facilities because people also order food. We could just go there."

Since Dr. Lowe was concerned that with Fenn as the Chair, he would have less control, I assured Fenn that just the opposite was true. With Fenn as the Chair, working closely with the President, Lowe would have more control, rather than less. From Lowe's point of view, Fenn should actually have been an advantageous candidate for this position: he was among the more moderate of our administrators, and would undoubtedly keep the radicals in check.

As the discussions among the faculty became more concrete, some of us decided to meet and draft our plans for a senate in writing. It did not take many sessions for us to reach a consensus on the rules governing the senate. We then called a meeting of all the faculty and eligible staff to finalize our plans. I think that everyone on staff who could be represented by the new Senate was there, and they endorsed all of our original plans. We decided to go ahead and give David Gidman, a widely respected member of the teaching staff, the chairmanship if Bob Fenn would not change his mind. Then, out of the crowd, came a voice, saying, "Sid, take one more shot at Bob."

I did not think I had much hope of changing Fenn's mind, but several other voices rang out, "Sid, do it!" Despite my doubts, I listened to the faculty, partly because I was pleased that there was so much interest, and partly because I felt the need to represent their views. I walked down the hall to Bob Fenn's office and repeated my earlier pitches. I also said, "If you persist in your present position, I think you will lose a lot of respect from the faculty. I will not pursue you further, however, since that is not my style." Bob heaved a substantial sigh, stood up, and walked down the hall with me to the room where the faculty was waiting. As we entered the room, there was a big round of applause, in which I enthusiastically joined. Our Faculty Senate was off to a good start. This body functioned very well, and, as one might expect, with the appropriate Dean serving as Chair, its business went forward much more smoothly than it might have gone otherwise. There were often disagreements between Fenn and the Executive Committee of the Senate as to the agenda, however.

An important event which threatened to disrupt our unity at Manchester was President Nixon's 1970 incursion into Cambodia during the Vietnam War. Thousands of people from across the country, including a number of Manchester students and faculty, immediately flocked to Washington, D.C. to protest this invasion. One of our faculty members who traveled to D.C. was Bob Vater, a music teacher who had been at the forefront of our campus solidarity activities. Neither Bob nor any of the other Manchester faculty had obtained permission for their absences, nor had they arranged for other faculty to teach their classes while they were gone. There wasn't much that could be done about the students who had cut classes for these events, but the actions of the faculty protesters posed a disciplinary problem for President Lowe.

The President wasn't the only one who had a problem with these teachers' unscheduled absences. Like the rest of the country, our campus was sharply divided between those who opposed the war and those who supported it. At Manchester, the hawks who supported the war were angry that some of our teachers had "jumped ship" to go on what they thought was an unjustified and unpatriotic jaunt to Washington. There began to be some talk on campus as to what would be a fitting punishment for these faculty "deserters."

The President called a Professional Staff Meeting to try to resolve some of the campus' differences over these political events. As at all of our other Staff meetings, we used Robert's Rules of Order. Though the Rules of Order can be very beneficial for more sedate discussions, they also can be cumbersome, and not always conducive to quick resolutions. The issue of unscheduled faculty absences naturally came up during the meeting. Tensions between the hawks and the doves were escalating, and I could hear that some of the discussions were starting to turn nasty.

I knew that if a quick resolution were not found, there could be deep wounds among the faculty which would have a lasting effect on interpersonal relations. I recalled what had happened to the Armenian community in the metal-working factories of New England after anti-Soviet incendiaries had murdered the bishop who was the head of the Armenian church in North and South America. The Armenians had already been divided prior to the 1933 assassination of Archbishop Leon Tourian, but, after his murder, Armenian-Americans split into two distinct pro- and anti-Soviet camps. Even though it would have been highly beneficial for Armenians in New England's factories to maintain their solidarity, their political differences caused them to pull apart. I had been trying to organize the metal-working trades in Western Massachusetts after World War II, and I had failed in every attempt to bring the Armenian unionists back together.

To prevent a similar split at Manchester, I quickly drew up a list of people evenly divided on both sides of the Vietnam War. My idea was that all of these people could serve on a committee to mediate and defuse the dispute over the unapproved absences. I showed the list to Bob Vater, and he made no objection. I then approached President Lowe during a break in the meeting, and said, "I have a plan to end this argument to the satisfaction of all the participants." I suggested that when the meeting resumed, I would rise and move to suspend Robert's Rules of Order for the rest of the meeting. Then the President would appoint the committee I had named to study the question and to propose whatever action they deemed necessary. I said to President Lowe, "If you don't like any name on this committee list, just tell me, and I will come up with a substitute. I chose these people because I think that they all are reasonable and that they would like to put this matter to rest." President Lowe agreed with my plan.

After the break, I made my motion, and it was unanimously passed. Lowe then announced the formation of the committee, with its charge. He also said that he was closing down the meeting until the committee adjourned, but that no one was to leave the premises until he declared that we were finished.

The committee met, and returned in a little over two hours with their proposals. As I had anticipated, they had come up with a solution to which everyone could agree. They suggested an amnesty for all of the faculty members who had previously cut classes, as well as a requirement that any faculty in the future who planned an absence from campus would observe the proper rules, such as finding other teachers to cover for them.

The hawks were mollified, the doves pleased, the President was put at ease, and the unity of the staff had been preserved. Both sides were happy, and acceptance of the committee's proposals was close to unanimous. Both the supporters and the detractors of the war had enough sense not to taunt each other at the close of the meeting, nor to let their disparate views affect their personal relationships.

Not too long afterward, in a hallway discussion, one of our members who was a practicing attorney said to me, "I finally have you figured out. You fight very hard for your position, and then you settle for what you can get." I replied, "You got it, Buddy!"

It wasn't so much my doing, however, that helped people at Manchester get along so well: it was really the quality of the staff who worked there. Some of the credit for this great staff should be assigned to Fred Lowe. He had been hired as the first president of Manchester when it was just a city college, and the funding for his salary had still been problematic. Clearly, he was a man of great principle. In 1966, shortly before I joined the faculty, Manchester voluntarily joined the newly-formed statewide system of community colleges—as did Norwalk, the only other city college in the state. My decision to apply for work at Manchester had been prompted by what I had been told by a friend who was also a friend of the Lowe family—that Fred was a staunch defender of civil liberties, and that, while he was a teacher, he had belonged to the American Federation of Teachers. I believe that Fred's reputation for fairness and open-mindedness persuaded a number of other fine faculty to find their home at Manchester.

As you might guess, it was very difficult for any president to avoid becoming assimilated by the bureaucratic systems of state government. Fred's leadership style was fine with me and the other campus activists as long as he was making the right decisions, but he was nonetheless pressured by all the deadwood in the system to rely on top-down management. Still, his heart was in the right place. Occasionally, when a group of us would remonstrate with him, he would pull open his suit jacket in a gesture of contrition and admit his guilt. No one had the heart to scold him too harshly. He was loved and respected by many people, including myself. His death of a heart attack in 1975 was a great loss, both to the college and to anyone who had known him personally.

Most of the staff at Manchester seemed to have very well-adjusted personalities, and many had interesting backgrounds, some in various fields of business. If mistreated by "the authorities," they were able to figure out what to do. In some cases, where appropriate, they were able to forget about the mistreatment, but, in others, they were prepared to stand on their own two feet and offer resistance. Overall, they were thoughtful people. With all of these qualities, they were ideally suited to teach in a community college. The students recognized this, and most of the teachers and other staff were admired by the student body. The Manchester staff fulfilled what I thought was their main role, which was to build up the self-esteem of their students by demonstrating their confidence in them.

In addition, many of my colleagues were strongly rooted in their communities. Many were active in their places of worship. It is interesting to note that a large number of the staff were participatory members of the Manchester Unitarian Universalist Society. Some were also involved in politics, mostly in the Democratic Party. The long-standing mayor of Manchester was a professor of sociology at the college.

Many of our faculty had Ph.D.'s or were working toward one. Manchester is only about 35 miles from the University of Connecticut at Storrs—not a difficult commute. I myself worked toward and earned my Ph.D. in the first five years of my employment at Manchester.

My office at Manchester was in a building that housed most of the teachers in the Social Science Division. I taught history, which I had always thought was a humanity rather than a social science, but, in any event, we all worked well together.

The teachers at Manchester were known as a great bunch of kidders, but it was always for fun and never out of mean-spiritedness. For example, the academic psychologists would often rib me for my devotion to Freud and to psychoanalysis. My reply was usually to urge them to read my dissertation, which had been published as a book, **Herbert Marcuse: From Marx to Freud and Beyond**. Or some teachers who lacked a Ph.D. would point out that holding that degree did not necessarily make one a good teacher, to which I would reply that having a Master's degree did not do that, either. In one situation, where I may have overdone it, a newly hired teacher got lost on the way to meeting a bunch of us for lunch. He was a teacher of geography, and I razzed him about it, saying such things as, "We had better change our hiring protocols when geographers can't find their way around." He was somewhat shocked, but after a few weeks, he came to understand our crew.

Among our crowd there was one man who was openly gay and one woman who was openly lesbian. They were fully accepted as part of our active core. I never heard a word of gossip or criticism about either one of them. This level of acceptance was something notable in those days, and says a great deal about the character of our staff.

I think the most spirited discussions in our early days were about freedom of choice in regard to the issue of abortion. Although tempers rose slightly during these discussions, they did not affect the cordiality and mutual respect of the staff for one another. On another potentially controversial subject, one Manchester professor was known to introduce irrelevant religious topics into his classes. This caused a few tsk, tsks by several faculty members, but the professor was nonetheless regarded in a tolerant fashion. I believe that the decisive element was that his students liked him. This was enough to remove any danger that some formal action would be taken against him. One interesting aspect of campus discussions about religion was that the President and the Dean of Faculty were both avowed atheists. We faculty always had a big laugh (to ourselves) when, in presiding over our annual graduation ceremonies, they both thanked God for our students' successes.

I was very comfortable in this environment. I had a strong sense of humor, along with a grab bag of what seemed like a million jokes. I was also able to roll with the punches. One question that arose later in my time at Manchester was who had the most seniority among our teachers. I thought that it was I, but the authorities decided otherwise. I never let this matter bother me, and never complained to anyone about it. The person named for that honor did not campaign for that designation, and he was in my department. I had received much approbation from my colleagues for my campus activism and my union work, and I did not want to diminish the honors that anyone else received.

I had good relations with practically all of my colleagues, and a warm relationship with many. My best friend at Manchester was Arthur Guinness, in the Business Division. He had been a sales manager for Dictaphone. When I met him, he was a fairly staunch Republican, but when he saw that many of the Democrats in the state legislature were very supportive of our budget, he gradually shifted to support their party.

Arthur Guinness and I both reacted dubiously when Fred Lowe suggested that all of the staff would benefit from participating in campus-wide encounter groups. In the late 1960's and early 1970's, many people around the country were infected by the encounter group bug. Encounter groups, so it was said, would allow people to let their hair down and have healthy discussions of the intimate details of their lives. Fred Lowe was enthusiastic about the idea because he thought encounter groups would improve relations within the college, and, as a consequence, would also improve our work.

Guinness went to the President, and tried to talk him out of the idea. He had seen some real-life examples of companies that had tried this method of developing business relations. All too often, the encounter groups had led to discontent among the participants.

I had some different concerns to discuss with Fred. From my reading, and from talking with people from various walks of life, I had realized that sharing more emotional intimacy than a relationship requires could lead to serious psychological consequences. In some cases, individuals who were ill-prepared to handle such intimacy had suffered psychotic episodes during or after encounter groups. I told Fred that if he continued with this idea, it would be advisable to have a psychiatrist nearby.

Unmoved by our objections, Fred went ahead and scheduled the compulsory encounter group meetings. I dutifully attended my appointed group. However, I knew what to expect, and thus was fully prepared to participate at a level with which I felt comfortable. If there were things about me which did not affect my job performance one way or another, I did not get into a discussion of them.

In talking over our experiences later, Guinness and I fully agreed that working relationships could and should be cordial, but that there was no need to go deeper unless someone turned out to be an especially good friend. We both thought that the following conversation could be repeated by two co-workers every day for thirty years, and still be highly appropriate:

"Hi, Charlie, what do you know?"

"Hey, Mac, save your money."

An interesting sidelight to the whole encounter group experience was related to me by a friend who was on the college's Advisory Board. She had been assigned to an encounter group that met at the President's home. She told me that, out of all the members in her encounter group, Fred Lowe was the least generous with any revelations about himself.

CHAPTER

2

Creating Statewide Coalitions

OUR EXPERIENCES ON OUR OWN CAMPUS CONVINCED THE Manchester activists that, in order to gain leverage and strength, we needed to create a unified organization of all the professionals in the community college system. Bob Vater was at the forefront of this movement, and I served as his aide. In 1966, the Board of Trustees of the community college system had come up with the idea of establishing a statewide faculty senate, and we supported this unifying move. We did not put forward any of our own candidates for positions on this senate, however, as we did not wish to create unnecessary friction between ourselves and management. In any case, no action on our part was necessary, since so many of the activists in our solidarity movement were recognized as outstanding individuals. On the basis of their merits alone, many of them were elected to the Senate, which met for the first time in January of 1967.

When a Republican governor, Thomas J. Meskill, replaced a Democrat in 1971, the need for statewide organizing became even more apparent. As soon as Meskill took office, he decided to solve the state's perennial budget problems by canceling that year's increments (annual pay raises) for all employees in higher education. This affected everyone from clerk-typists to college presidents. The most unfair part of Meskill's decision was that he had not applied a similar cut in pay to other state employees. It was only the employees in the state's institutions of higher education who were going to lose their increments.

Bob Vater and I worked with Bill Dowd–a very active member at Manchester—as well as other Manchester people to try to get various organizations in higher education to do something about Meskill's decision. Vater and Dowd, who both had been involved in American Federation of Teachers locals when they had worked in the public school system, contacted the leadership of the AFT and of the Connecticut Education Association (CEA). I spoke with leaders of the American Association of University Professors (AAUP) but to no avail. We three then came up with the idea that we would join ranks with the University of Connecticut, the four state colleges, and the four technical colleges to collectively sue the state and the Governor. To carry out this plan, we created an organization called HELP, the Higher Education Legal Program. Kay Bergin, a professor of secretarial sciences from Mattatuck Community College, was selected as the first Chairperson of HELP. We met with Kay, and decided that Bob and I should go forth to raise money for HELP, with the goal of hiring a good attorney. We had set our sights on Attorney Burton Weinstein, a prominent lawyer in Bridgeport, Connecticut who was known for his work on civil liberties cases.

Before moving full speed ahead with our fund-raising, I decided to test the waters. My business-owner father had always told me that everything has a "natural price," or a price that everyone can agree is appropriate. The founders of HELP had decided that a contribution of $10 per person was the natural price for getting our increments back. Including myself, there were five members of the History Department at Manchester. In a few minutes, I had collected $50 from our department alone.

I then shared my experiences with some activists in the community college system. As a boy in the early 1930's, I had learned a great deal from watching the United Jewish Appeal raise funds in my home town. There were about seventy Jewish families in Northampton, Massachusetts at that time. The vast majority of wage earners for these families were merchants. There were also a few doctors, lawyers, and dentists.

In the early thirties, there was a tremendous need in the Jewish community to raise large amounts of money for the rescue of Jewish families from the menace of Hitlerism in Europe. The local committee of the United Jewish Appeal would meet and decide on the quota that each family should contribute. To determine the amount for each merchant, all one had to do was count the number of employees in his or her shop. (Each employee's earnings were roughly equivalent to the others'.) The quotas were high: they were set at $1,000 per employee. My father, who had five people in his employ at his shoe store, was on the organizing committee. The committee would visit each wage earner in the family and let him or her know what their "assessment" was.

In their visits with the families, the committee members would educate people on the situation in Europe, offer details of the rescue attempts, and answer any questions. I don't think any shouting ever took place. The visitation group members had a strong point in their favor: they had all made their own contributions. They did not permit any chiseling. If someone's quota was $5,000, they would not settle for $4,400. The only exception was that donors would be allowed to make their payments over time, as long as everything was fully paid within one year. If the committee did not get a commitment for the amount they requested, they left courteously, asking the hoped-for donor to reconsider his refusal. Of course, the issues at stake were enormously compelling: in the face of the Holocaust, contributors were highly motivated by the life-or-death appeal.

My observations of these fundraising methods informed my behavior when raising money for HELP. Another item in my bag of tricks was my understanding that reestablishing our increments was not only a matter of conviction, but one of self-interest—for the present, and for the future. I instructed our fundraising committee members to be calm and patient, but, under no circumstances, were they to allow anyone to make less than the required $10 contribution. The committee could tell members how many people in their college had contributed, but they could reveal no names. And since management on each campus was also about to lose their increments, we included them in our appeal.

At Manchester, we raised $880. Only three people demurred. We did not make their names public, and we did not threaten them that we would do so. It so happened, however, that when I was standing outside with some of the people from our HELP fundraising committee one beautiful spring day, they spotted the three people who had not committed to give. They asked me to approach one of the delinquents. I walked over to him and said, "I don't know why you did not contribute to our fund (actually, I did know: he was opposed to unions) and I am not going to harass you about this. That's not my style. But sooner or later, it's inevitable that it will leak out—not from me, but from others—what you did not do. You will lose some friends. However, it's up to you." He reached into his wallet and gave me $10, for which I gave him a receipt. I returned to the group, and people were amazed. "How did you do it?" they asked. "In my usual way," I said. "It was just like the way I sell shoes. I acted from my first approach that he would do his part, and he did."

From this can be learned a few lessons about raising money. It is important not to bully or threaten people, but, rather, to explain. It is also helpful to act confident, though not cocky, that you will get what you are asking for. I used these precepts to help fundraising committees on several campuses achieve their goals for HELP. Even formerly timid people came to enjoy raising money.

We filed our complaint in court in November of 1972, but it took a full year for our suit to come before Judge Samuel Goldberg at the state Circuit Court in Middletown, Connecticut. I had heard from several people how interesting the personal and legal interchanges in the trial were, but I had been too busy helping the case along to see and hear the fun. So, one day, I decided to go and see for myself.

As I mentioned earlier, ours was a class action suit filed by the various professional employees from the state's two universities, the technical colleges, and the community colleges. Our lawyer was excellent, but he had not fully prepared one of the faculty members from the University of Connecticut. This professor testified that he had been recruited by UConn from the University of Michigan, and although he had been told that the annual increment would not be a fixed portion of his compensation, the increment had, to his knowledge, always been given each year. In other words, he had come to UConn for the money (hardly a crime).

When Judge Goldberg asked the professor his current salary he had to confess that he did not know. This is a common failing among college teachers: all they know is that their salaries are not enough. Then the professor said, "Oh, wait a minute. I got paid today, and I have my pay stub with me." He drew the stub out of his pocket and consulted it for what seemed like an eternity. He could not figure it out. Judge Goldberg got impatient and demanded that the witness show him the stub. He couldn't figure it out, either. I am always a closer on union deals, and I also got impatient. Uninvited, I called out, "Take the number in the upper right-hand corner and multiply it by 26.1. That will be his annual salary." The judge took my advice, but he also rebuked me soundly for speaking out of turn. I was lucky that he did not cite me for contempt; I should have asked if I could approach the bench to see if I could be of help. It was an interesting day.

Unfortunately, we lost our suit on the basis of a well-established notion in Anglo-Saxon law—that the King can do no wrong. The idea was that we could sue the state only if the state agreed that we had the right to file such a suit. We probably had made a mistake to file our complaint in a state court: if we had done so in a federal court, we might very well have had a different outcome. Personally, I thought I got my ten buck's worth when I heard the news that a sheriff had served a subpoena on Governor Meskill as part of our suit.

Years later, I was in a popular restaurant with a group of friends when former Governor Meskill walked in. I hesitated for a few minutes, but then walked over to him and introduced myself as one of the people who had sued him over the increment question. "That's OK," he said, "everyone was suing me in those days." In the years since he had left the governorship, he had gone on to an appointment as a judge in the Second Circuit Court of Appeals in New York State. "I hear you have been making some very fair decisions in favor of appellants in employment law cases," I told him. I had my information on good authority. Dan Livingston, our union's lawyer at that time, had shepherded some appellants through Meskill's court.

After getting HELP off the ground, Vater and I looked around for new worlds to conquer. We then came up with the idea of CHEC, the Connecticut Higher Education Coalition. The purpose of CHEC was to gather together all those who wished to advocate for higher education in the political arena. We set up a committee with delegates from the University of Connecticut, the state university, the technical colleges, and ourselves. The technical college teachers and the state university people did a good job in executing the agenda of this committee, but the UConn people lagged behind. They were, after all, the fat cats of the public higher education system.

The CHEC committee decided to call a large meeting to protest Governor Meskill's attempt to cut the higher education budget. We rented a large meeting room at the Hilton Hotel in Hartford, and we sold tickets at $5 each for roughly 1100 seats. We had our people personally contact legislators from across the state to come and be our guests. Homer Babbidge, the president of UConn, was selected as our main speaker, and the response of our legislative guests was heartwarming. The entire atmosphere and the rousing reception given to President Babbidge encouraged him to later run for governor in a primary. Although he had a great deal of support from educators, he did not quite make it.

The most important outcome of the positive meeting at the Hilton was that the mood of gloom and doom from which we had all been suffering was dispersed. Many legislators were newly inspired at that meeting to stick up for progressive programs, and their determination gave us a terrific boost in morale which lasted for several years.

After the meeting ended, Vater and I were mobbed by well-wishers who correctly perceived that we had been the initiators of a very positive event. When things had quieted down, I retired to a friend's house for a couple of drinks. My right hand was so swollen from being enthusiastically pumped that it took two sinks full of ice to return it to something like its normal size.

What had we accomplished? We had pushed forward our agenda for the appropriate support for higher education. In so doing, it became apparent to the naysayers that all was not lost. It also became clear to Bob and me that we needed to form a statewide union if we were going to strongly oppose efforts to shortchange education's best interests.

CHAPTER
3

How Even Smart People Can Be Fooled

BEFORE I CAN CONTINUE WITH MY STORY, I NEED TO GO BACK to the time when I was an undergraduate at the University of Chicago, and did something that both helped and hurt me in my subsequent teaching and union work. The year was 1939, and I was recruited by a friend I admired a good deal to join the Communist Party. He was older than I, and had a wealth of experience in the workplace and in unions. He had previously been a reporter for one of the nation's best newspapers, the St. Louis Post-Dispatch. Since he came from a working class background, he was greatly sought after by all the leftist groups on campus—the Socialists, the Communists, and the Trotskyites. Many of the students at the University of Chicago had parents who worked as schoolteachers, accountants, librarians, or at other "petit bourgeois" kinds of jobs, but since his father was a coal miner, my friend was a real honest-to-God proletarian. (You cannot always be sure what the designation of proletarian means, however. My friend once came to a party with a girlfriend whose father he described as a coal miner. His girlfriend was wearing a full-length mink coat. Her father was certainly a coal-miner: he owned the mine.)

In that time and place, being a Communist was not that unusual. There was a group on campus associated with a journal entitled, **Science and Society**, a Marxist journal with strong leanings toward Communism. Many of my friends were Communists, or Communist sympathizers. I liked them, and wanted to spend time with them because they were lively in spirit, well-educated, and open-minded. Importantly, I did not see any evidence of anti-Semitism or racism among the Communists I had met, and I was in agreement with their goal of elevating the working class.

Since I was perceived as an effective "mass leader," I was immediately put to work by the Party. Before joining up, I had been one of the founders and leaders of a student group protesting a proposed tuition hike. In a campaign modeled after the collective bargaining campaigns of the CIO (Congress of Industrial Organizations) we had collected from fellow students 1100 cards which assigned their collective bargaining rights (non-existent) to our committee. These signed cards represented about 10% of the student body. The Communist Party was very desirous of working with people who could conduct a spirited campaign such as ours. I was placed in the Party unit at the University where great care was taken that no informers had joined our group. The others were placed in the YCL, the Young Communist League, where a lower level of security was maintained. Even though the national persecutions under McCarthyism had not yet reared their ugly heads, there was still considerable secrecy surrounding membership in the Communist Party. Many Americans were frightened of the Party, and its alleged connections with the Soviet Union.

After I was graduated from the University in 1940, I worked as a partner for a couple of years in my father's shoe business in Northampton, Massachusetts, while at the same time continuing my outside work for the Party. In 1941, I married my first wife, who was also a Party member. I then took a course in machine shop work, and worked for a few months as a milling machine operator and a set-up man. Finally, I was drafted, and entered the Army in June, 1943. Naturally, as with all other Communists, my connections with the Party were severed during the time I was in the Army. While I was on furlough in 1944, however, I helped set up a committee of independent voters in Northampton to work for the reelection of Franklin Delano Roosevelt. I went overseas in 1944, and served in France as a clerk typist and interpreter for an ambulance battalion. I was honorably discharged in January of 1946.

When I returned to Northampton, I explored various employment possibilities, and decided to re-establish my partnership in my father's shoe business. I worked in that position until December of 1946, when the Communist Party asked me to become the full-time organizer of their Western Massachusetts district, at a barely subsistence salary. Despite the financial sacrifices involved, my wife completely supported my decision to accept the job. We and our two young sons moved to Springfield, where I became a more important contributor to the Party's work. In 1947, the city committee of the Party decided to place me as a candidate in the race for alderman. I received 2.2% of the total votes cast for that office.

For years, I had little difficulty with the "Party line," which was for the most part dictated by Moscow, although

I was largely unaware of that fact at the time. Some of the work we did was highly commendable. I was particularly proud of the fact that the Communist Party in Springfield was at first the lone voice demanding that the city hire African-American bus drivers. I also felt good about the fact that, through my work in the Party, I offered some useful advice to union organizers in various factories in the Springfield area.

Beginning in 1947, I began working with friends and Party members to elect Henry Wallace for president of the United States on the Progressive Party ticket. Wallace, who admirably advocated putting an end to segregation and establishing universal government health insurance, was regarded with suspicion by many mainstream politicians because he also held fairly permissive views about Stalin and the Soviet Union. I convinced many activists within the Democratic Party to run for office under the Progressive Party banner, and thus unwittingly brought to an end several promising political careers. I still regret this. In 1952, Wallace was to explain in his book, **Where I Was Wrong**, that his former support of the Soviet Union had been based on inadequate information about Stalin's murderous rampages.

For myself, I passed off claims against the Soviet Union as "capitalist propaganda." I knew from personal experience that many of the American newspapers at that time, controlled by the publishing empire of William Randolph Hearst, featured reports about unions that were largely untrue. I also knew that Hearst had been pro-Nazi during the 1930's, and had at various times used his newspapers to fan the flames of hatred against targeted countries and minority groups. There was little reported in his papers that I trusted or believed.

With the advent of Joseph McCarthy's anti-Communism campaigns, any pre-existing national distrust of Communists was intensified. In 1951, as the political atmosphere worsened, I was requested by the Party to lay low for a while, and to leave New England. My second wife—also a Party member—and I spent almost a year on the West Coast, living and working under assumed names. We returned to New England in 1952, and lived in Rhode Island, still under assumed names. My wife worked primarily as a secretary, and I held a number of positions as a machinist. We also participated in the local Party organization, I as a regional organizer for southern New England, and my wife as a liaison with the New Bedford organization. In January of 1953, I quit my machinist job to devote myself to Party work full-time. Also in that year, my wife and I noticed that we were under surveillance by the FBI. We decided to move to Boston, and I was assigned a position as the Boston organizer, eventually using my real name.

Both my wife and I were subpoenaed to testify in September of 1955 before the Massachusetts Commission to Investigate Communism, also known as the Bowker Commission, after the Commission's chairman, Massachusetts state Senator Philip Bowker. We both stated to the Commission that we would be happy to defend our beliefs in any public arena, but that we would not discuss our views or our associations under compulsion before any McCarthy-like investigating committee. I did state to the Commission that neither I nor those with whom I had been associating "have ever advocated any form of subversion. I abhor the use of force and violence."

The FBI surveillance did not decrease after the Bowker

Commission hearings. If anything, it deepened. On May 29, 1956, as chance would have it, the FBI arrested me as I was leaving the hospital room where I had been visiting my wife and newborn daughter. I was indicted under the Smith Act for conspiring to violently overthrow the U.S. government. Unlike many of the other people who had been charged under the Smith Act and who had to do considerable jail time, I was fortunate to spend only one week in jail. My wife's mother, a socialist, paid to bail me out. In 1957, the U.S. Supreme Court decided that many of the Smith Act convictions were unconstitutional, and the charges against me and the other Massachusetts Smith Act defendants were dropped.

After my arrest, I made a decision to leave the Party, although the two facts were unrelated. Since I knew that it would look like I was abandoning my "comrades," I did not reveal my departure publicly until the Smith Act cases were resolved. My decision to leave the Party was based on two major political developments. One was the 1956 Soviet invasion of Hungary to suppress the Hungarian Revolt. This invasion led to the downfall of the legitimate Imre Nagy regime, and, in the end, to Nagy's execution, along with hundreds of other reform Communists. I found the Soviet Union's suppression of the Hungarian Revolution to be abhorrent, and in direct opposition to the democratic ideals I espoused.

The other major factor in my decision to leave the Communist Party was the so-called secret speech of Nikita Khrushchev, delivered at the 20th Congress of the Soviet Communist Party in 1956. In that speech, Khrushchev revealed for the first time that Stalin had been a brutal despot who had been responsible for violent purges, extreme nationalism, and anti-Semitism. I was aghast to hear these admissions. I was equally disturbed by what Khrushchev did not say. Every formal address to a Party Congress had hitherto started with a long survey of the international political situation—understandably, since the USSR was under the threat of suppression by leaders of the European countries. In his secret speech, Khrushchev said not a word about the current international situation, undoubtedly because of the political repression in Hungary which the USSR had perpetrated.

As Isaac Deutscher pointed out in his biography of Stalin, that dictator is best understood as an Asiatic tyrant of the old school. Here was a man who had never visited any country in Western Europe, and yet was dictating policy to the Communist Parties of European countries. For example, Stalin's orders to the KPD, the Communist Party of Germany, were based on his faulty assessment of fascism as the last gasp of industrial capitalism. Underestimating the growing strength of the National Socialist German Workers Party, Stalin promoted the idea that the KPD would take power after the Nazis had faded away. In the month's preceding Hitler's accession, Stalin's advice led many rank and file comrades to run around Berlin and other major German cities, painting with whitewash on convenient walls, "Nach Hitler, uns." (After us, Hitler.) He should have advised them to write, instead, "Hitler nach uns" (Hitler is after us) thereby possibly saving the lives of many German Communists and other anti-fascists. Some of the wiser KPD leaders had publicly dissented from Stalin's extremely stupid policy, but to no avail.

For me, one of Stalin's worst crimes was his despicable betrayal of the Spanish Peoples' Republic in the 1930's, and his use of aid to Spain to cover up his organized assassinations of those, especially the Trotskyites of the Workers Party of Marxist Unification (POUM) whom he considered his enemies. Stalin had disingenuously promised help and support to the anti-fascists in Spain, only to secretly plot the destruction of their republican government. The efforts of the Spanish republicans to combat the dictator, General Franco, in 1936 were sabotaged at every turn. Thousands of Spanish patriots and idealistic young people from around the world who had joined their cause lost their lives in a fight that was undermined by Stalin from the start. It later became known that Stalin had also plundered the treasury of the dying Republic by swindling the anti-fascists out of millions of dollars in arms deals.

My feelings of betrayal when I learned of Stalin's plots and violent repressions were bitter indeed. The loss of my blind idealism, however, would later help me become a better teacher and a more realistic activist. It is also true that through my work with the Communist Party, I had gained valuable public speaking and organizing experience. I had become accustomed to educating people about political and class issues, and had discovered that teaching was something I enjoyed. However, I eventually came to describe my long detour through Communism in these terms, "When I joined the Communist Party, I checked my brains at the door. When I left, I picked them up again."

After I left the Party, I never saw any of my Smith Act co-defendants again, nor any of the other Party activists I had known. For about 18 months, I devoted my spare time to trying to uncover where I had gone wrong. I wanted to know why I had allowed myself to be drawn into the

Communists' circle, and what had attracted me to their movement in the first place. I read all kinds of material which, while not banned by the Party, was frowned upon as improper reading for a devoted Communist. One of the books that explained the most to me was **Darkness at Noon** by Aruthur Koestler, which described his own disillusionment with Communism and his break with the Party. The works of the Russian anarchist Viktor Serge were also very helpful to me, as were the writings of Leon Trotsky. Trotsky was steeped in European history, and could have added a great deal to Stalin's understanding of international affairs, but that madman was too preoccupied with his own schemes to pay much attention.

Decades after I left the Party, I traveled to England with a friend who had helped me figure out how to get to Highgate Cemetery, where Karl Marx was buried. My friend was no Marxist, but she knew something of my feelings, and how disappointed I would be if I did not get to visit his grave. We started off on a bus, then took a taxi, and then had to walk across a wide field. I was just beginning to suffer from arthritis, but my friend urged me on, and we finally made it. Someone had already been there to pay their respects, and had left a bouquet of garden flowers tied with a red ribbon. Tears came to my eyes, and my friend discreetly stepped back to allow me my personal grief. Marx, of course, had not been to blame for the excesses of Russian Communism. I sometimes said to my Western Civilization classes at Manchester Community College that the history of three great Jews—Marx, Freud, and Einstein—explained the intellectual history of the entire 19th and 20th centuries. In my view, Marx was a great Promethean figure of the 19th century.

CHAPTER
4

The Founding and Development of the 4 C's

I N OUR PLANS TO CREATE A STATEWIDE UNION OF COM-
MUNITY college professionals, Bob Vater and I faced
a large stumbling block. Many of the staff in Connecticut's community colleges were past or current members of various national teachers' unions, and many had
participated in other unions in non-educational settings.
The organizations with the greatest representation on
our campuses were the American Federation of Teachers
(AFT) and the Connecticut Education Association (CEA)
but these unions were bitter rivals in the public school
system. If we were to choose to affiliate with one of them,
it was likely that our members would become embroiled
in their constant internecine struggles. As soon as one of
their contracts expired, the AFT and the CEA competed
to win representation rights for the school system's employees. Their battles turned out to be seesaw events: first
one would win, and then the other. Their struggles for
domination were huge time- and energy-wasters for their
members. Witnessing this counterproductive process
prompted Bob Vater and I to campaign for the creation

of a new, unified organization which would be independent of the existing unions. We gradually converted the Manchester staff to our point of view, and then worked on persuading the staff of the other community colleges.

The statewide faculty senate proved to be instrumental in fostering acceptance of the idea of an overarching union. In late April of 1973, the Senate for Connecticut Community Colleges passed a motion to hold a constitutional convention the following month to form a new umbrella organization. At the constitutional convention on May 24, the Senate for Connecticut Community Colleges ended its own existence and reconstituted itself as a union called the Congress of Connecticut Community Colleges—with a mandate to form a new, statewide faculty senate within three months. The purpose of the Congress was to represent the interests of all Connecticut community college teachers and professionals. This new union achieved the unity we had wanted, but also defended an individual's right to belong to any other group he or she wished. We had learned that in order to establish a successful new organization, it is important to not force people to give up their former loyalties. Our low dues structure of $13 per year would allow people to hold memberships in more than one union.

Until officers could be elected in the fall, the Congress was run by a Steering Committee, with Bob Vater selected as the Steering Committee Chair. I continued to serve as Vater's aide. About fifty staff members from the various colleges participated in meetings throughout that summer, serving on committees and drafting documents that outlined the Congress' position on matters of importance to its members.

Our new union was apparently created not a moment too soon. Five days after the Congress' founding convention, the community colleges' statewide Board of Trustees issued a working draft of a new personnel policy, along with a timetable that provided for faculty reaction and then Board adoption within one month. Not only was this timetable unrealistic with so many faculty leaving for the summer, but the substance of the document was authoritarian and undemocratic to an extreme. The Steering Committee of the Congress rejected the new personnel policy in its entirety and requested that the Board of Trustees negotiate with the Congress to formulate a new set of policies acceptable to the colleges' professional staff. At the same time, the Congress sent the Board a copy of its newly drafted constitution, along with a Statement of Professional Dignity, and a document we entitled, **A Program of Action**. Our new organization was off and running, and our positions and those of the Board could not have been farther apart.

On September 29, 1973, the first full meeting of the 4 C's elected Bob Vater as its first president. We elected a number of other officers, as well, including a first Vice President to represent the interests of faculty members, and a second Vice President to represent the members who worked as administrators, counselors, and librarians. The Congress also created a number of key committees at that time. The Legislative Committee was assigned the task of meeting with gubernatorial candidate Ella Grasso to seek her support for a collective bargaining bill for state employees—something that Connecticut sorely lacked.

There is a standard process by which a union becomes legally certified and recognized, but without a collective bargaining law for state employees on the books, the Congress unfortunately could not take all of the necessary steps. For two years after its creation, the Congress could engage only in what is known as *de facto*—without the authority of law—collective bargaining with the Board of Trustees. The Board claimed that our sporadic meetings were simply "meeting and discussing." Without the backing of a collective bargaining law, the rule of each college president and the Board's overarching control were extremely arbitrary and sometimes even degrading. Each college president, for example, could and often did make up his own rules for the granting of promotions and tenure. Even though we were a majority organization—by early 1974, we represented 69% of the eligible people in the community college system—we had very little legal recourse in our struggles for fair and equitable treatment.

It had become increasingly evident that reform was needed in the community college system. A master plan drafted in late 1973 by the Connecticut Commission on Higher Education had proposed that the state colleges and the University of Connecticut would receive more money per student than would the community colleges. As reported in the 4 C's newsletter of December, 1973, this formula "was based on the assumption that it is more difficult to teach upper division students and graduate students." The Congress responded to this proposal with a strongly-worded statement that pointed out the myriad ways that such a formula failed to support equality of educational opportunity.

State budget cuts were also a constant danger. In early 1975, the state Budget Office asked Dr. Searle Charles, the then-Chair of the Board of Trustees, to prepare a report on the impact of cutting $1.1 million from the community college budget. Dr. Charles replied that the budget could not be cut by more than $725,000 without jeopardizing degree programs. The Board then asked the presidents of the community colleges to examine their course offerings to see which classes could be combined or cancelled. Apparently, the administration of one of the community colleges had reacted to the threatened cuts by placing an advertisement in a local newspaper, asking for volunteer teachers to "help teach such subjects as History, English, Italian, Music, Biological Sciences, Psychology, etc." When Bob Vater got wind of this notice, he immediately protested to Dr. Charles, who promised to ensure that the offending advertisement would be removed.

Reform, or at least personnel changes, were needed on individual campuses, as well. In 1975, Fred Lowe stepped down as president of Manchester Community College and then, sadly, passed away. He was quickly succeeded by Ronald Denison. The contrast between Denison and the civil libertarian Fred was distinct and painful. During Denison's first year in office, I was still technically Bob Vater's aide, but I was away on sabbatical as a post-doctoral fellow at the University of Chicago. In the spring, Bob called to tell me about some of the goings-on at our college. It had become apparent to him that Denison had been systematically going through the personnel files of the entire staff at Manchester, identifying and then clandestinely harassing people whom he thought were potential troublemakers. Denison's suspicions fell on, among others, a teacher named Jim who had strongly opposed the war in Vietnam. Prior to coming to Manchester, Jim had been employed at Trinity College, and had lived in a tent on campus to demonstrate his protest. Jim, and others like him, began to receive hang-up calls during their office hours, presumably to see whether they were at work when they had said they would be. The President also began requesting copies of class reading lists from various division directors. The faculty at Manchester were alarmed that Denison would try to censor their choice of reading material for their students.

The application which I had filled out when I applied for work at Manchester, and which all state employees in Connecticut were required to complete, had contained a question which read, "Have you ever been arrested?" Later, a widespread movement of state employees convinced the legislature that that question should be changed to, "Have you ever been convicted?" Naturally, I supported this revision, although I was not part of the class action that produced the change. As is common in employment applications, the penalty for telling a lie anywhere on the form could have been dismissal from my job. In my application, I had therefore stated truthfully that I had been arrested under the Smith Act in 1956, but that my record had been cleared the next year by a Supreme Court decision.

As I mentioned earlier, one reason I had gone to work at Manchester was that a friend had told me about Fred Lowe's ardent defense of civil liberties. I knew from the same friend that Lowe had read my application for state employment and that he was aware I had given up my connections with the Communist Party in 1957. Denison, of course, had access to the same information in my personnel file.

A couple of weeks after my conversation with Vater, I received what I had been expecting: a phone call so clumsy that I knew it must be from the FBI. Posing as an interested reader of my book about Freud, Marx, and Marcuse, the caller wanted to know if I was aware of any meetings dealing with the subject of social change. I referred the person to the bibliography in my book. Almost twenty years after the charges against me had been dropped, the FBI was still hoping I would reveal to them the names of other radicals. It was clear to me who had re-awakened the FBI's interest in my case, and when I returned to Manchester late that summer, I was forewarned and forearmed.

By that time, I had been granted 50% released time to perform my union work as Vater's aide. Denison tried to monkey around with this grant. I went to talk to him alone (the Congress' lawyer had no problem with that, knowing that I would not incur a liability for either the union or myself). The president was seated on a platform which he had had built to raise his desk about five inches off the floor. He was a relatively short man, and thought that the platform would give him an advantage. Most of the chairs in the college had been made by inmates in one of the state's prisons. His was one of these, and could be adjusted by rotating the chair higher. One day, at the start of a meeting, Denison rotated his chair so high that the seat came off, and he fell on the floor. Not today, however.

Denison opened the discussion by saying, "I have great admiration for the people of Israel. They have built up their country politically and economically, while all this time the Palestinians across the river have been lazy and have done nothing." I replied, "Mr. President, I am not a Zionist, although in 1948 I took a bus trip to Washington, D.C. from Northampton, Massachusetts to support the establishment of the state of Israel. And if I were in Israel today, I would be a member of that segment of the population protesting the ban on the intermarriage of Jews and Arabs. That issue of civil liberties is no different in substance than the reason I am here today." I later told a bare-bones version of this story to ten people, five of whom, including my father, were Jewish. Without prompting, they all said, "this guy is an anti-Semite." Incidentally, Denison backed off from his efforts to curtail my released time.

A control freak, Denison caused considerable protest among the Manchester staff. To quell the objections, he initiated a series of four meetings with the academic divisions of the college. There were many people, I had heard, who had spoken up about their discontent at these meetings. My division, Social Sciences, probably had the largest group of staff who were opposed to Denison's methods. At our meeting with the President, several of my colleagues spoke before I took the floor. As I talked, I moved to the front of the room and stood by the teacher's desk. I spoke in a calm voice and a respectful manner (respectful of the position, not of the man).

Denison did not like what I was saying. He tried the door against the wall where he sat, but it was locked. To leave the room, he therefore had to pass directly in front of me. I said, "Oh, you cannot meet me head-on in a battle of ideas, can you?" As he walked by me, and then out the door, I called out "Coward!" five times in a steadily rising voice. I don't see how anyone could recapture the esteem of a crowd after slinking away like that.

The same year that Denison was hired, a law was finally passed that legitimized collective bargaining for state employees. Once this law was on the books, we still had no contract, but we could then rely upon the protective precedents established by the Wagner Act of 1935. This Act had two important provisions: one was that workers and management must sit down together to discuss their needs and come to a mutual agreement and the second was that these agreements had to be set down in writing. In other words, both parties must come under the rule of law, rather than the rule of the monarch. For labor organizers, one could compare the Wagner Act with the Magna Carta in England, or even with the discovery of the Holy Grail.

When I returned from the University of Chicago, the Congress began collecting signed representation cards that would give us the right to bargain on behalf of our members. Prior to the card collecting, we had conducted a long conversation among ourselves about choosing a national union with which to affiliate. Affiliating with a national union would give us greater clout and far greater financial support.

As I have mentioned, many of us in the 4 C's had a pre-existing allegiance to the AFT or the CEA, but we wanted to find a new group with which to affiliate, one untainted by the representation battles and the psychology of the past. We eventually decided to ally ourselves with AFSCME, the American Federation of State, County, and Municipal Employees, a moderate union with many members in state employment. AFSME represented workers in many types of employment, including a number of blue-collar jobs. We did not rush our members into a decision to join forces with AFSCME, since we understood that what we were talking about was, in fact, a minor revolution. Ultimately, our members were convinced of the suitability of the affiliation, and, in September of 1975, we made the move without leaving any scars. The fact that our affiliation with AFSCME was to be for a trial period of one year (or until a contract was negotiated with the Board, whichever came first) made the arrangement easier for our members to swallow.

A number of people on the outside were shocked by our decision, however, partly because of AFSCME's association with blue-collar work, and in part because Vater had been in the AFT convention caucus that had elected Al Shanker as its president. Dozens of calls from AFT stalwarts poured in, but Vater held firm. He had personally experienced the futility of the constant battles between the AFT and the CEA, and he wanted to make a fresh start. AFSCME it was, and we cut a deal with them that was advantageous to us both. We guaranteed AFSCME a quick victory to help them win over a broad section of state workers; in exchange, they would give us $60,000 in cash for our election campaign. Both sides kept their share of the bargain, and, for around 18 months, the 4 C's was known as the Congress-AFSCME.

With AFSCME's backing, the 4 C's conducted a very successful push to gather representation cards from our members. In the first week of our campaign, we collected cards from 81% of the faculty and professionals in the state's community colleges. We needed only 35% of the members to sign up in order to have an election, but our goal was to get 100% of the cards signed. In the next week, we increased the amount of signed cards to 91%. On October 1, the first day that the new collective bargaining law went into effect, we became the first group of state workers to file collective bargaining cards.

The next step in the process of recognition of our union was unit determination—where it would be decided, under the direction of the state Labor Relations Board, exactly whom our union would represent. For us, this phase entailed a series of meetings between the 4 C's and the representatives of the Board of Trustees. People from the Connecticut State Employees Association (CSEA) initially participated in our meetings, since they had submitted some membership cards to the Labor Board for their consideration. Membership cards were useless for labor representation, however, since they did not conform to the requirement that the individuals who signed them must indicate that, in so doing, they were assigning their bargaining rights to a union. The membership cards were eventually thrown out. Before they were proclaimed to be worthless, however, I and a lawyer hired temporarily by the CSEA conducted an interesting exchange.

This lawyer was snooty and overbearing in his demeanor. I had written out individual file cards, totaling probably 750, for anyone who had administrative duties in any of the community colleges. One person in that group taught archaeology at Norwalk Community College, and his additional duties involved being a digmaster. The CSEA lawyer asked, "What's a digmaster?" I sat up straighter in mock surprise. "You have the effrontery to come here and claim that you are able to represent professional employees, and you don't even know what a digmaster is?" Bob Vater was sitting next to me. He leaned over and whispered in my ear, "What's a digmaster?" I explained to Bob later what the teacher from Norwalk had told me, that a digmaster is someone who supervises an archaeological dig.

The Congress and the Board of Trustees agreed right off the bat that there should be one unit for all twelve of the state's community colleges, rather than each college bargaining as a separate unit. From our point of view, a single unit would give us more strength, and be less chaotic to manage. From management's point of view, a single unit was advantageous because it would prevent various competing factions from continuously upping the ante of the benefits or salaries they could receive.

We wanted wall-to-wall organizing, meaning that we wanted a union that represented everyone who worked in the community college system, including clerical workers and maintainers. We did not get our wish: the Labor Relations Board ruled that there would be a separate statewide unit for all clerical workers, as well as another statewide unit for all maintainers. This ruling was based partly on the large size of each of these groups: there were about 11,000 clerical workers statewide and about 9,000 maintainers. Unfortunately, the Labor Board's decision was not helpful to these workers, who, for the most part, were scattered in small groups of three to ten across the state. Their large numbers and their geographical placement made it difficult for their parent unions to serve them well. The Congress, with its many activists in twelve locations, would have had a much easier time helping them. Many of these workers were to tell us later that they wished we could represent them, but there was nothing we could do.

After settling this matter, our discussions focused on every professional position in the system. We had requested that all of the deans in the colleges be assigned to the Congress; we did not expect to win this point, but it was part of our psychological warfare to ask for it. Also, a denial of this request might help us win something else, since the Labor Board appeared to be evenhanded in its decisions. It was obvious that we would get all of the teachers—which we did—along with all of the department heads.

We were better prepared for these meetings than were the Board of Trustees' representatives. As I mentioned, I had a file card with information for every teacher who had any administrative duties whatsoever. With many of our assertions, the Board of Trustees reps had to run upstairs (we were on the first floor) to the Board's office so that they could call the college involved, and check on our facts. We were never proven wrong. We would have applied to include the college presidents in our union, if we had thought it had been at all possible to get them. In our view, the presidents had no real power, and time proved that they were indeed often overruled by the Board on decisive issues.

Frustrated that they could not get the department chairs into the category of management, the Board conducted a furious battle to win on the question of the academic division chairs. In each college, there was one academic division chair for each of the four divisions: social sciences, biological sciences, physical sciences and mathematics, and the humanities. The Board also fought to keep in management the nursing directors in each of the five colleges that had a nursing program. I could never figure out why the Board was so gung-ho to win on the nursing directors. My best guess was that they might have known that two or three of these five were not sympathetic to labor. In any case, the Labor Board assigned them to us, along with the division directors.

The 4 C's also had a strong interest in organizing part-timers—those employees who worked less than twenty hours per week. We wanted to represent them for two reasons: one was that, in the event of a strike, we did not want them to be tempted to serve as scabs, and the other was that by bringing up the low end of our wage scale, we would benefit every worker in the system. There was a large barrier to our including part-timers in our union, however: at the time that the 4 C's was recognized, state labor law did not allow part-timers to bargain collectively. Because of this, no part-timers received benefits. It was no coincidence that there were an inordinate number of employees in the state system who were hired to work for 19 hours per week. As many as 10% of the total community college faculty and staff were stuck with these hours. We therefore joined a statewide coalition of organizations interested in advocating for part-timers, and, finally, after a decade of persistent lobbying, we were successful in getting the law changed. We then organized the part-timers, and when the special election was held, again under the aegis of the Connecticut State Labor Relations Board, we had an easy victory—as did many of the other state employees' unions.

Many tasks had to be accomplished before we could reach that point, however. First and foremost, the 4 C's had to win a representative election. To establish a place on the ballot, any challenger would have needed collective bargaining cards signed by only 10% of the members, but despite furious efforts on their parts, none of the other unions were able to accomplish this.

Some people within the 4 C's whom we privately called our Psychological Warfare Group advised that we ask the Board of Trustees of the community college system to recognize our union before the election, knowing that they would refuse. I have found that sheer nerve is an important aspect of psychological warfare. Obviously, management had its own consultants, and I did not have any problem with that. I never contemplated working in such a position myself, but, if I had, I would have advised the Board of Trustees to recognize the 4 C's forthwith. That is, unless I had suspected that the signed cards were phony. As it turned out, they were not. When the election to establish our union was held in December of 1975, the vote was 91% for the Congress-AFSCME and 9% for no union. Had the Board of Trustees recognized us before the election, the management of the community colleges would have won our respect. (So, they were clueless. So, do me something).

In labor elections, it is very unusual to achieve a vote that is as high as the amount of representation cards that were initially signed. In many industries, this is because there can be considerable pressure and intimidation exerted by management against potential union members after they sign up. People become frightened, and back away from their original commitments. In our situation, however, many of our members were experienced union participants who were hungry to regain the advantages and protections of union representation that they had experienced in their former jobs. Not only that, I suspect that the community colleges' Board of Trustees did not take our movement seriously enough to consider us a threat. If they had, they might have tried to dissuade our members from participating fully in our election.

Once our union had been officially recognized, we had to bargain for our first contract for our full-time employees. Contract negotiations with representatives of the Board of Trustees began on January 6, 1976. Our negotiating team was led by Donald Pogue, the 4 C's attorney, and also consisted of Bob Vater and myself, John Blake from South Central Community College, Barbara Dolyak of Housatonic, Margaret Owens of Manchester, Ray Marafino of Greater Hartford, and Alice Letteney of Quinebaug Valley Community College.

Over 59% of our new hires in the community college system had come from the local public schools where, for years, they had enjoyed the protections of working under a contract. Of course, our members were interested in making more money, but, far more urgently, they wanted a contract which would provide a more level playing field with management. Our members were also deeply interested in being more involved in the democratic governance of the community college system. They wanted more say in the choice of curriculum, the development of new programs, and in the selection of department heads and division directors.

One of Bob Vater's strengths as a leader was that he genuinely wanted, and invited, democratic participation from the Congress' members. He wasn't interested in power for power's sake, but wished instead to accurately represent the interests of his constituents. To that end, in early February of 1976, he sent to all the 4 C's members a detailed listing of our proposed contract clauses, requesting their input, along with a questionnaire, asking the members to indicate their priorities on a list of possible wage increases and fringe benefits.

Throughout the negotiation process, Bob's efforts to keep our membership informed and involved were reinforced both by leaders on the 12 campuses, and by the 4 C's strong Executive Board. Our first Executive Board included Bob, me, and Seranne Quish from Manchester, Margaret Brown and Ada Lambert from Norwalk, Kay Bergin and Ray Cacciatore from Mattatuck, Martha Flint from Housatonic, Gene Tito from South Central, and John Makrogianis from Middlesex Community College. Among the many other campus leaders of note were Wyley Peckham and Harry Cunha of Middlesex, Susan Logston of South Central, and Gil Jackson of Norwalk.

Bob and the 4 C's activists made sure our members knew when and where to apply political pressure to the negotiation process. It was a 14-month-long, weary struggle to win our first contract: when all was said and done, we had met 91 times with the Board's agents. Throughout the agonizing delays, our negotiating team remained constant in its willingness to entertain any serious proposals from the representatives of the Board. Unfortunately, until threats of job actions and embarrassing unfair labor practice charges forced the Board to begin negotiating with us in earnest, such serious proposals were far and few between.

What we did receive, instead, were a number of empty promises, and—worse yet—proposals that actually would have undermined any progress we had attained in previous years. This latter tactic, known in union circles as "dropping the floor," was meant to demoralize us and force us into a position where we would have wrongly imagined that we would have to beg for even the smallest of concessions.

It is instructive and sad to read in Bob's bulletins to our membership how his cautious optimism changed first to bewildered groping for a charitable explanation for the Board's obdurate behavior, and then to outrage over the Board's persistent delays and stonewalling. Bob and I knew that in order to force the Board into a meaningful dialogue, we would have to maintain our unity as an organization. The Board knew this, too, and, in a last-ditch effort to break our resolve, they began in late 1976 to circulate misinformation and bogus change-in-representation cards to our members. If our membership had not been so focused, savvy, and well-informed, there could have been a danger that these false rumors and equally false petitions would have disrupted our negotiations. As it was, the Board's underhanded actions formed the basis of a second set of unfair labor practice charges which we filed against them in 1977 with the Connecticut Labor Relations Board. One of our charges was that the employer or its agents had circulated petitions that would have served as a basis for decertification of our union, all the while communicating to our members that the state and the employer would approve of such decertification.

Our members were too sophisticated to fall for such ploys. Their parents and grandparents, through their participation in the AFL-CIO, had inspired in many of them a strong understanding of the value of an independent labor movement. Walter Reuther, the progressive leader of the United Auto Workers., was a role model for a goodly number of our people. They also were well-acquainted with picket lines. Moreover, for nearly four years, we had kept them apprised of every step as we had moved from an unrecognized entity to a recognized union. We had urged our members to strengthen their ties with their state legislators, and we had called upon them to participate in demonstrations to support the collective bargaining law. There would be no stopping them now that we were so close to having a contract. When called to action, our members repeatedly turned out in force. Our slogan: "We want a contract, and we want it now!"

A turning point in our struggle was when our members voted to authorize a strike. The strike vote meeting was held in a church not far from the Board of Trustees' office. Since he thought I was an effective speaker, Vater designated me to make the appeal. It was an impassioned speech in which my major theme was that we, the 4 C's members, had built the community college system to its present strength, that we were the ones introducing new programs—not the managers of the system. In other words, that the system belonged to us.

According to the 4 C's constitution, strike votes and affiliation votes had to be conducted by secret ballot. To count the ballots, we chose only those people whom we knew were highly regarded by their colleagues. The vote was 424 to nothing, in favor of a strike. We achieved this unanimity both by inspiring our members and by telling them honestly that in Connecticut strikes against the state were illegal, that some people would go to jail, and that we would have to guard against members weakening in their resolve over what might be a long process. In other words, we were perfectly candid with our members.

The strike vote turned up the pressure on the Board. Now, even the state would not tolerate the Board endlessly dragging its feet. The legislature set a deadline of April 1, 1977 to receive our negotiated contract. With the

Board's full knowledge, we planned a system-wide job action for March 30, asking all of our members to request a full personal day off to attend an important Congress meeting. With nearly 100% of our members committed to participate, this would effectively shut down the system. Our plan was to place before our members the complete contract proposals of both parties for acceptance or rejection. Frightened by our show of strength, the Board authorized a half-day leave for all of the community college professional staff, but we maintained our plan to take the full day.

As the end of March drew near, our negotiating team worked feverishly, trying to negotiate an acceptable contract to deliver to the legislature by April 1st. Miraculously, the same Board that had found itself unable to come to an agreement with us for 14 months suddenly found the will to decide on the crucial issues it had been avoiding. Our first contract was negotiated, and we used the March 30th date for a ratification meeting.

Over 400 members attended the ratification meeting, a very high percentage of our total of approximately 650 members. We met in the gymnasium of the Greater Hartford Community College, and the excitement in the room was palpable. Our chief negotiator, attorney Donald Pogue, arrived with a copy of the Board's version of the contract language. A quick reading of the document uncovered what we believed were some errors. Pogue went immediately to the Board's offices upstairs, where the ambiguous language was resolved in about thirty minutes. When he returned, he was holding the contract high over his head. We spent a few minutes explaining the document and answering some members' questions.

Then we voted. When the ratification was announced, the crowd went wild. Vater turned toward me, and hugged and kissed me. A few days earlier, he had announced to me and our Executive Board that he would be retiring as President of the 4 C's, but now he whispered, "I think I've changed my mind." I replied, "We'll talk about it later." I didn't want anything to spoil the pleasure of the meeting. I believe that no one who was there ever forgot that moment: I know that I never will. With our members' help, we had produced a nearly flawless campaign.

People have asked me how the 4 C's garnered so much support from the bottom up. It was because the rank-and-file members trusted us as leaders. For years, they had seen us unafraid to represent them without a union, and thus without a strong defense against our possibly being fired. They saw on most of the college campuses a vigorous defense of their rights. They also saw that their leaders were not bleeding the 4 C's funds for personal advantage, but were, in many cases, using their own money to travel around the state on members' business. Our operation was also as financially transparent as it possibly could be. Our finances were reported publicly eight times per year and were available, not only to our members, but to anyone else who was interested.

More importantly, we always took the high road. We were extremely strong defenders of the short- and long-term interests of the community college system. Most of our members, and all of our leadership, fought a determined legislative battle for the proposed community college budget each year. With twelve colleges all over the state, we could, and did, produce hundreds of advocates for our system's needs.

Our devotion to our work was not fake. We were strong believers in the idea of the community college, and our very presence at the colleges was proof of that. Many of our members, such as myself, had left better-paying jobs to work in the community college system. I had left a $16,000 per year position for my $6,000 per year teaching job at Manchester. A majority of our new hires were lured away from the public school system—and not for the money. These recruits for the community colleges usually represented the best of public school employees. They had given up their recognized positions, along with the protections of seniority and tenure, to venture down this new road. They did this out of principle. They believed in the accessible education offered by community colleges. (I wish the same could have been said about some in the management group).

Community colleges were founded to extend the advantages of an affordable college education to people in or near their own communities. They offered a two-year degree in career areas such as business management, law enforcement, and the health professions, as well as degrees in liberal arts for students who wished to continue their education at a four-year college or university. One of the purposes of community colleges was to help people who were the most economically vulnerable—women, the poor, and minorities—move from unskilled jobs to positions that commanded higher salaries. Community colleges thus exercised a democratizing influence on society, and helped to raise up less advantaged members of the labor force.

As part of the growing community college movement, the 4 C's was at the forefront of progressive legislation.

We developed and monitored a mentoring system to help people of color obtain full-time teaching positions in the community colleges. We welcomed women into the leadership of our organization, both on individual campuses and at the statewide level. When we first organized the 4 C's, the membership was roughly one-third female. Within ten years, women were in the majority of our members. We also vigorously defended student rights. These were not things that we did sporadically: we were committed to promoting equality on an ongoing basis.

We did not accomplish this through high-blown speeches. We believed in, and practiced, leadership by example. Briefly put, we achieved a very high level of *esprit de corps.* Compared to the University of Connecticut, we were at the bottom of the totem pole in terms of salary and working conditions, but our value to the state and to our students was very high. What we did, in essence, was raise the self-confidence of our members and of our students.

CHAPTER
5

Changing of the Guard

WHEN BOB HAD ANNOUNCED THAT HE WOULD BE RETIRING as President of the 4 C's, he had explained to me and to the union's Executive Board that he did not think that union work was exciting enough, and that he wanted to do something more radical. He continued teaching at Manchester, and served for a number of years as the chairperson of the 4 C's Grievance Committee, but he also got himself elected to the city of Hartford's Board of Education, and later became its President. If you can figure out how that is more radical than doing union work, please let me know. In any event, as President of the Hartford Board of Education, Bob played a major a role in obtaining for the teachers' union an excellent contract in 1985 that was the envy of AFT locals throughout the country. This contract was part of his overall plan to improve the public school system in Hartford. Sadly, the tremendous struggle to attain this model contract undermined his health, and he died prematurely of a heart attack in 1988.

Bob Vater was a great guy, and an unforgettable character. He served the 4 C's well and with great courage. He had an infallible political sense, and could always tell how the membership would think on any important issue. In addition, he was a wonderful jazz pianist, and an inspiring figure for his students. He had played in jazz clubs all over New England to considerable acclaim. One time, at an AFSCME party to celebrate their hoped-for addition of prison guards to their union, an orchestra was playing, and there was a good, but empty, dance floor. This was unusual for a union party. Bob went up to the band leader, and asked if he could sit at the piano for a while; the band leader agreed. Within five minutes under Bob's leadership, the band had come to life, and the floor was full of happy dancers. True, Bob was also extremely impetuous, and was not always the easiest person to work with, but the executives of our system were so unimaginative that they were not able to fully utilize his talents. The same was true for many other 4 C's members.

Bob's announcement that he would be retiring took me by surprise, but then I accepted it, and decided that I was the logical candidate to replace him. The constitution of the Congress provided that if an officer were to leave before his or her term had expired, the union's Executive Board would then appoint a replacement to serve out the rest of the term. Once the term was completed, there would be an election. Since I wanted the Board to make me their appointee, I talked to each of the Board members individually, asking for their support for my presidency.

Then Bob made that remark to me at the ratification meeting about changing his mind on retiring. I arranged to talk with him privately about his decision, and told him that, not knowing that he was going to reconsider, I had spoken with each of the Executive Board members about my interest in the position. I also told him calmly that several of the Board members had expressed strong reservations to me about his leadership style. They felt he was too volatile, and too aggressive with union members who disagreed with him. I told Bob truthfully that I did not join in their remarks (though I secretly agreed with some of them). I simply told the Board members that they had been able to observe me in action for some years, and that I thought they could see my leadership style was quite different from Bob's.

I suggested to Bob that if he really wanted to change his mind about retiring as President, then we should call a meeting of the Executive Board and ask them to take a vote between us. I said, "I am your friend, and I am not going to attack you in such a meeting, and I am sure that you will not attack me. I will make it clear to the Board, as I am to you now, that if they want you to continue as President, I will return as your aide, if you wish, and will serve you just as faithfully as I have for the past six years." Bob said, "Let me think about it, and I'll get back to you tomorrow." He decided that he did not want to participate in such a meeting and that he was out of the picture as far as being president of the 4 C's. Since I had made such a favorable impression on the Board, and since no one else expressed an interest in the position, I was duly appointed President of the Congress.

When it came time for the election a few months later, I was unpleasantly surprised to learn that Bob had encouraged another candidate to oppose me. His name was Jack McLain, and he had played a very positive role in helping the 4 C's win its electoral victory. He had also written a fine pamphlet arguing the good and bad points of affiliating with a partially blue-collar union such as AF-SCME, but supporting our overall positions. We had liked his pamphlet so much that we had distributed it to all of our members.

When Jack's candidacy became known, I invited him out to dinner. I asked him how much union experience he had had in his previous job. He said that he had served as the grievance officer in the high school where he had taught. I told him very frankly that I didn't think he had the necessary experience to be President of our union, but that if he wished to support my bid for the presidency and follow me around as my aide for the next two years—and we both agreed he had learned enough to become the President—I would retire and support his candidacy. Jack politely declined, and withdrew from the race. Opposed by a financial aid administrator who received less than a sixth of the vote, I was swept into office. I was subsequently elected for nine more two-year terms, bringing my total time as President to a little over eighteen years. Despite some problems with his leadership style, Bob had been a very fine president for our incipient union. I had merits of my own. I was very methodical in my research and preparation of necessary material. I was also patient when dealing with troublesome union members. I never yelled at them or at our staff, although Sonia Berke, my "right-hand person" and I often had heated arguments, sometimes about union policies, but most often about the writing of all kinds of documents. But even our bluster had certain limits. Kit Collette, the Congress' administrative assistant, once said she was surprised that after sessions where Sonia and I had yelled at each other, we would calm down and say, "Where are we going for lunch today?"

Sonia was the first professional full-time staff member whom Bob and I had hired, and a very fortunate choice it proved to be. She and I had each earned our Master's degrees from Trinity College in Hartford. We both also earned our Ph.D.'s in history from the University of Connecticut, specializing in Western European thought. We met for the first time in a UConn class on medieval English history. Sonia turned out to be a great editor and writer, and she edited both my dissertation, and the book taken from it. I later paid her back by typing the first draft of her entire dissertation.

Sonia had done some excellent part-time work for the 4 C's before we were recognized as a union. When she performed a task, it was not necessary to check it over: we knew that it would be right. In 1976, when it came time for us to decide on a full-time staffer, the choice was between Sonia and another part-time person whom we had hired to help create a new unit of non-teaching professionals at the University of Connecticut. I was bemused to learn, after the fact, that Sonia had thought the other candidate would get the nod, since the other person was more radical politically than she. Sonia was an Adlai Stevenson Democrat (a liberal Democrat.) Our choice was not made on the basis of any candidate's radicalism, however, but on whom we thought would best serve our members.

When Sonia was in high school, she had decided that she wanted to become a lawyer. She was an excellent student, and she won a prestigious scholarship that would have paid for her tuition at any college in New York state. She wanted to go to Cornell, and then to Cornell Law

School, but her parents preferred that she live at home. She ended up attending a very good school—Barnard College—but she was greatly disappointed that she was never able to study law.

Her work with the 4 C's perhaps offered the next best thing. With every new contract, she insisted that I sit down and answer all of her questions, since she did not want to have to say to any member who telephoned, "Wait a minute while I ask Sid." Over time, as she gained knowledge and experience, Sonia began to participate in grievance hearings, later even handling grievance sessions by herself. She also participated in negotiations with members of the Board's central office staff. Because of her strong communication skills and her devotion to the union's members, we felt comfortable entrusting even the most serious cases to her.

She was warmly admired by and friendly with both men and women in the 4 C's—no mean feat, at times. Her job often involved working with lawyers, who listened to her carefully, and who treated her with a great deal of respect. No wonder she later said that her years at the Congress were among the happiest of her working life.

Sonia and I were both very interested in language. For many years, she and I co-wrote all of the Congress' written material, which included letters, leaflets, and a monthly newsletter. She also participated in reviewing the language of all of our contract proposals. Sonia and I had an efficient way of working together. I would dash off a leaflet in thirty or forty minutes, and she would re-work it in about two hours. On her own, she could have produced a leaflet in a little over three hours: the main difference between our writing styles was that she always generated perfect prose the first time around. Each of her sentences logically followed the preceding one, and all the parts formed a coherent whole.

Sonia rarely made an error with regard to language, but one time she made a funny mistake. A 4 C's member sold office supplies and he wanted us to buy his products. His prices were good, and I gave Sonia the go-ahead. Most of the people in the office used pens, but she did all of her writing with a number two lead pencil. The salesperson asked Sonia how many pencils we needed, and suggested a gross. No, said Sonia, make that a dozen gross. The only problem was, Sonia didn't realize that one gross meant twelve dozen, or 144 pencils. She had therefore ordered a grand total of 1,728 pencils! After my initial shock had worn off, I laughed and told her that her punishment would be that she could not resign from her job until all of those pencils were gone. She retired in 1995, at about the same time I did, when there were only sixteen pencils left.

Every year, the 4 C's ran a leadership conference for our members with a full day, or more, of seminars and workshops. The conference also featured an evening banquet, free to all members, attended by around 400 people. Sonia and I would go over every detail of the banquet beforehand, asking ourselves if we had enough parking, if we needed to rent coatracks, and the like. We also spent a lot of time planning the menu. We tried to introduce people to a new menu item each year.

When I retired in 1995, Sonia organized a large surprise party for me, inviting not only 4 C's members, but government officials, leaders of other unions, and members of my family. The party was a complete success. Sonia told me afterwards that she had wanted to plan such an event without my help just to show me that she could do it. Another pleasant retirement surprise were words of appreciation from a number of our members, printed in the **Congress Chronicles**, the 4 C's newsletter. One remark in particular made my pulse race faster, "It was because of you that we all could stand a little higher."

In the day-to-day business of our union, I was always ready to listen to the complaints or problems of our members, but, even so, some of them were hesitant to talk with me. Those who understood how organizations worked would sometimes talk to Sonia first. If she thought they were on the wrong track, she would tell them, but she would otherwise urge them to talk to me. If they were still reluctant, she would say, "Let me talk to Sid. I'll see what I can do." This would not arise very often, but Sonia would occasionally feel the need to tell me I had been too hard on a member, and that the person deserved another hearing. She would urge the member to talk to me again, and assure the person that she had prepared the way by speaking with me first. What employer could ask for anything more?

Perhaps some people were hesitant to talk to me because I had a reputation for being tough. I believed in toughness, and I could work with others who were tough themselves. But the toughness I most admired was on the inside, not on the outside. Occasionally, in dealing with difficult people in management, however, I would enjoy letting loose.

I felt it was important that I also be a conciliator. I was very conscious of the need to maintain unity among our base, and the positions I took on issues were guided by what was needed to keep us together. I also wanted to convey the feeling that faculty were collaborators with management, not merely serfs. Bob Vater had believed, and I agreed with him, that the faculty should even have a dominant say in the selection of college presidents, but since our Congress members did not support that position, we kept our mouths firmly shut on that issue.

Unless I was being abused in some way, I treated management with respect, even though some members of that group did not deserve it. I remained clear as to our aims, and concentrated on achieving them. In particular, I realized that I had to constantly keep my priorities in order, so I spent some time reviewing, and sometimes reprioritizing, my aims every week.

Of course, I had my own weaknesses as a leader. One of them was that I did not give people sufficient praise. After this was pointed out to me, I tried hard to change, and did, in fact, do so. My new habit of praise included complimenting our members and the union staff in public announcements.

I realized when I thought about it that my parents had not been given to offering praise. As a child, if I came home with a report card with straight A's, the most they would ever say was, "That's nice." In a sense, this was a sort of praise. They simply expected that I was going to do well. After all, my mother and her sister had both been salutatorians of their respective high school classes, and one of their brothers had been the valedictorian. My father was a successful businessman and civic leader. My parents' thinking, which I suppose was natural enough, was that I would follow in their footsteps.

Although my father never praised me to my face, I

heard from a cousin who often lunched with him and some other men that my father frequently praised me to that group. I finally concluded that my father was incapable of praising me directly.

I believe that my parents' attitudes helped develop in me a determination to do things on my own, and, more importantly, to satisfy myself that I was doing well and not worry about others' perceptions of me. I set very high standards for myself, and fortunately, was usually able to meet them. I also learned that a little public boasting was necessary in the fiercely competitive world of unions.

Although I judged myself by elevated standards, I think my standards were realistic when it came to the administration of our union contract. I was very logical when figuring out how much the Congress could get and how to get it. It was easier to think more clearly when I was not mentally besieged by unrealistic expectations.

Because of my strong communication skills, I was a creditable advocate and was convincing both to our own members and to anyone who sat on the other side of the negotiating table. I could easily construct a scenario from smoke and mirrors which would put a contract settlement in the best possible light. What that means in plain language is that our settlement offers were not hard to swallow.

I was reasonably familiar with labor law in Connecticut and elsewhere. From reading legal decisions and the arguments used to reach them in higher education cases all over the country, I had gained considerable knowledge of contract language. From this body of legal material, many precedents could be found to demonstrate that our proposals were, in fact, part of the mainstream. My own know-how on these issues was enhanced over the years by the services of our two extremely competent labor attorneys, Don Pogue and Dan Livingston. If they didn't know something, they would research it and find the answer.

The union benefited because I was also a very hard worker. I once kept track of my hours for the union over a three-year period. An arbitrator would have designated 20 hours released time per week for my union work. My records showed that I worked an average of 46 hours per week for the 4 C's, except for two weeks' vacation every year. It often turned out that I performed union work seven days per week. I felt it was necessary to work so many hours because the needs and problems of the union were very great. In a typical day at the 4 C's office, I was in meetings all day long with union members, chapter leaders, our staff members, and our lawyer. My lunch break, usually taken with Sonia, was essentially another meeting to update each other on the union's most pressing concerns. I was not paid for any of my union activities, although the Congress did provide me with an expense account of $6,000 per year. Most of that money I spent on travel to our twelve member colleges.

Because I received released time for my union work, I had to teach only two classes, rather than the usual four. I did not shirk my responsibilities in that area, and tried to improve my teaching every semester. I suppose I was lucky in this regard. Some of my best lectures were composed in the thirty-nine minutes it took me to drive from my home to the college. I enjoyed sharing my knowledge with my students, and I cast my lectures in language that I thought they could understand. I agreed with my colleagues who argued that if you could not explain a topic in language that the average person could understand, you did not fully understand the subject yourself.

When I eventually retired as union president, I left the Congress with one million dollars in liquid assets from our investments. And I do mean liquid. We could have picked up the telephone at any time and told our broker in New York to sell everything. Within ten days, we would have had the cash in our hands. Since our annual budget was $650,000 per year, we could have operated for one year and four months without collecting any dues whatsoever—which some shortsighted members wanted us to do. As you can guess, we did nothing of the kind, since we were not itchy to get our hands on the cash for our own self-interest. The money was all for the defense and offense of our members.

Sometimes our members would request my help with matters that were not covered by labor law. For example, long before the Americans with Disabilities Act was created, various members asked me to help them find accommodations for their disabilities. One such request was from a chemistry teacher who had developed post-polio syndrome, and who was afraid he would lose his job unless he could find a way to move around his lab to prepare his classes. I enlisted support from his college's management, and found a way to pay for a motorized scooter for him. I was also able to find the money for a similar scooter for another member who suffered from post-polio syndrome. I never told anyone about this, but word got around. Perhaps it was for this reason that I became known as a helpful guy to whom our members could talk confidentially about their personal problems.

I helped our members not because I wanted to build

up our union, but out of a strong sense of social responsibility. In one very sad situation, one of our members was suffering from a fatal disease, and was on his deathbed. There were some problems with his retirement account which would have reduced the pension his wife would have received, and we filed a grievance on his behalf. I could not budge Jackson Foley, however, who was the attorney and chief negotiator for the community college system's Board of Trustees.

I went to talk to Foley privately, face to face. I expressed dismay that someone with his background (he was the son of a minister) could fail to help a member in such a dire situation. I then told him about my father who had, over the years, bought out competing shoe stores in Northampton. My father liked two of the salespersons who had been with one of the stores for a number of years, so he took them on as his own employees. One of them, Frank Harvey, unfortunately developed cancer four or five years after my father hired him. In those days, retail clerks did not receive health insurance as part of their compensation, and Frank's family found that they could not continue to make the payments for his hospital care. His wife brought him home, and nursed him there until he died, around six months after his diagnosis. My father paid Frank his full salary until the end, and would have paid it to him for as long as he had lived. To me, the most important part of this story was that, rather than simply sending Frank's family a check every week, my father would go every Saturday night (payday, in those days) to bring Frank his money in person. He would spend some time chatting with Frank and his family, and offer them his usual encouraging words.

Jack Foley was abashed when he heard this story, and quickly gave in. We settled the grievance and wrote up a copy of the settlement that day. With our lawyer in tow, we rushed to the hospital, where our member's wife was fortunately in attendance. We explained the terms of the settlement to both of them, and our member signed the agreement. We accomplished this in the nick to time, because four days later he was dead.

An important postscript to the story of my father's social conscience was that, at his funeral, a young woman came up to me whom I did not recognize. "I am Frank Harvey's daughter," she said, "and I came to express my family's gratitude for everything your father did for us."

Some founding members of the 4 C's receive certificates of appreciation (left to right): Sid Lipshires; Bob Vater, the union's first president; Kay Bergin, former president of the statewide faculty senate and Second Vice President of the 4 C's; and David Gidman, a leader of the statewide faculty senate.

Unidentified community college students and staff, protesting state budget cuts.

Unidentified student shows support for faculty demands at a 4 C's rally.

Sid Lipshires, holding sign, with members Jim Zagroba (left rear), Dorian Wilkes (middle rear) and unidentified activists at a 4 C's protest in Hartford, Connecticut.

Four C's staffer Sonia Berke; Sid Lipshires; and Don Pogue (right), the union's first attorney, outside the State Capitol in Hartford.

Dan Livingston, the union's second attorney, at a 4 C's arbitration hearing.

Sid Lipshires, in a lighter moment, at a 4 C's Christmas party.

CHAPTER

6

Denison Deposed and other Necessities

OVER THE YEARS, OUR ATTACKS ON MANCHESTER'S PRESIDENT Denison contributed to the denial of his expected increment for the ensuing academic year. Despite his knowledge that the increment had been denied, he instructed Tony Borkowski, Manchester's business manager, to cut him a check for the full amount. Tony at that point was not a strong supporter of the union. He had the notion that a worker should always obey the boss. I found out what Denison had done, and confronted Jack Foley. "How did you find this out?" he demanded. I replied, "Haven't you learned by now that there are no secrets in public employment?" Jack then informed me that the Board of Trustees was planning to take some action against President Denison, placing a reprimand in his personnel file so severe that any future minor infraction would lead to his dismissal.

Every few days whenever I saw Jack after that, I would say, "Nu?" explaining to him that this Polish-Yiddish word meant, "What's happening?" The Board of Directors finally did dismiss Denison in 1979, but as so frequently happens in this topsy-turvy world, they also gave him a favorable recommendation which enabled him to get a good job in the Midwest. I went back to Jack, full of indignation, and told him that the Executive Director of the Board had let it be known that anyone who had had a problem with Denison would be welcome to go to him and discuss what he knew. I pointed out that the only management person who had taken advantage of this offer was the Assistant to the President, who occupied the lowest position on the administrative totem pole. None of the deans had spoken up, even though they had intimate knowledge of Denison's misdeeds. To make matters worse, the Board had turned around and blamed Tony Borkowski for the whole affair: I had heard they were preparing a harsh letter of reprimand for him. I said to Jack, "The Board's plan to blame Tony for the entire dismal increment mess can only succeed over my dead body."

I only used the expression, "over my dead body" twice in my entire thirty years of activity at Manchester. Jack knew that I was serious and that, in addition, the union of which I was president had recently reported that we had $670,000 in liquid assets. It was clear that we had the financial wherewithal to launch for Tony a vigorous defense. The grievance which we filed on Tony's behalf caused the harsh reprimand to be downgraded to a mild slap on the wrist. He subsequently became a strong supporter of the 4 C's.

A couple of years after Denison was ousted, the Congress took some rousing actions alongside other state employees to save the 35-hour work week. The popular Democratic Governor, Ella Grasso, had proposed increasing the state workers' week to 40 hours. When she resigned for health reasons in December of 1980, her Lieutenant

Governor, William O'Neill, took her place, and continued to support all of her proposals.

In February of 1981, state workers had set up a picket line to protest this issue outside the Democrats' annual Jefferson-Jackson Day Dinner at the Hartford Hilton. The Manchester activists were out in full force. Bob Vater had gone to a second floor window inside the Hilton, and, until the hotel's security officers dragged him away, was yelling encouragement to the crowd below. When Joe Fauliso, O'Neill's new Lieutenant Governor, directed his limousine down an access road to bypass the protesters, Arthur Guinness left our picket line in hot pursuit. I will never forget the sight of Guinness, his face contorted with rage, as he ran alongside the slow-moving Cadillac. He was shaking his clenched fist while repeatedly shouting, "SCAB, SCAB!"

A few months later, I had an interesting experience in connection with the same work-week-increase problem. The state employees' unions had called for a lunch-hour protest meeting on the lawn of the state Capitol and had urged the attendance of those who worked nearby. When I arrived at the meeting, there were about 2,500 people present, and a light rain was falling. It was on the same day that Mehmet Ali A ca had attempted to assassinate Pope John Paul II, and a number of portable radios were blaring away.

I immediately called an impromptu meeting of the heads of all the state unions. I made a couple of points. First, we had to get the radios turned off. Then we had to calm the crowd over the issue of the Pope. If we could not do that, then we would have wasted a day, as well as our efforts to mobilize the employees who worked close to the

State Capitol. I was on the speaker's list for the meeting, but was not near the top. I offered to speak first unless someone else wanted to do so. The majority of the state union leaders were Catholic, but they seemed content to allow me to step forward even though I was a Jew and was not particularly religious.

The organizers had obtained the use of a beat-up car and a hand-held microphone. This set-up was not ideal. It would have been better if there had been a pickup truck with the usual sound equipment, and a ladder so that the speakers could easily climb into the back of the truck.

The meeting's organizers had received permission to stand on the hood of the car, which by then was quite slippery in the rain. I took off my shoes, and a couple of guys helped me get up on the hood. The first thing I did was to ask the owners of the radios to shut them off. I told the crowd that the union leaders had a radio playing softly nearby, and that if any definite news came out, we would immediately alert the crowd. The next thing I did was ask for a minute of silent prayer for the safe recovery of the Pope.

I then made a rip-roaring speech attacking the Governor's plan. I got the expected enthusiastic response. I was still standing on the hood of the car, waiting to pass the microphone to the next speaker, when Don Pogue came up to me and said, "That was a great speech. I didn't know you had it in you." I looked at him, gave him my thanks, and climbed off the car. I said to myself, "I've worked with you for over five years, Don, and you still don't know who I am or how I operate." I knew that Don considered himself to be a general of the working classes, but, as the Jewish mother said to her son was who posing in a white uniform with plenty of gold braid in front of his new boat, "Son, by your poppa you're a cap'n, and by your momma you're a cap'n, but by a cap'n you're no cap'n."

Eight years later, Don left his law firm since he needed more income to put his two daughters through college. He was first appointed as Chairman of the state's Commission on Hospitals and Health Care, and then, in 1994, was appointed as a judge in the state's Superior Court. At the founding of the 4 C's, he and Vater and I had made a solemn pledge to stick with the 4 C's forever. We did not go so far as to slice our thumbs and seal our oath in blood. As you can see, for one reason or another, I was the only one of the three of us to honor that pledge.

Don and his wife had gone to Yale with Bill Clinton. I had a little joke about Don which I shared with a few friends when we heard that Don hoped for an appointment from Clinton to a federal district court. (It turned out that he didn't get the appointment he wanted, but had to settle for an appointment to the United States Court of International Trade.) My joke went like this: what were the last words that Don spoke to the President on his recent visit to Washington? The answer was, "Zaidele, bench mir." This was a play on words, based in part on the Passover Seder where a glass of wine is placed on the table for the Prophet Elijah, who is referred to as "Little Grandfather" or Zaidele. The youngster who had asked the Four Questions at the Seder, also then has the duty of opening the front door, and saying, "Zaidele bench mir," or "Little grandfather, bless me." Bench, or course, is a pun, since a judge is said to sit on a bench.

I attended Don's inauguration as a judge, and, over the years, attended several other functions in his honor. He had acquitted himself as the 4 C's attorney very well, and we at the Congress had learned a great deal from him.

When Don left, we went for a year without a General Counsel, and then decided to hire another lawyer from Don's former firm. I had talked often with Dan Livingston, and I chose him because he had presence. By presence I mean that when he walked into a room, people understood that he meant business. Vater had created that impression also, but he felt that he had to strut a little to let people know he was there. Vater was a real general of the working class, however.

CHAPTER

7

A Challenge to the 4 C's

I N 1982, DURING MY THIRD TERM AS PRESIDENT OF THE 4 C's, support for our union ran from moderate to very high in eleven of our twelve colleges. The weak spot was Mattatuck Community College in Waterbury. Mattatuck was a large college with a very good activist as its leading force. This activist, after serving for two years as my aide, had been elected in 1981 as the Vice President of the Congress' "ACL's," or Administrators, Counselors, and Librarians.

The 4 C's had never bothered to establish a credit card for itself so we frequently used my personal credit card. Clearly, this was a mistake. Our Vice President was given my card for union business, but then decided to use it to finance a trip for his family, as well as to buy four new tires for his car. In essence, he was thumbing his nose at us, and this created a crisis in our union. We began to pay particular attention to working with people in the Mattatuck chapter, and learned that our Vice President was very much in control of the goings-on there. He did a great deal for the members of his chapter, and used a clever personal technique to ensure the loyalty of his base. His method? A noontime poker game of several years' running for anyone who wished to participate.

Of course, we had to remove him from his 4 C's office. This led him to try to displace our union as the representative agent. There was no possibility that the Labor Board would allow a single college to establish itself as an independent bargaining agent, so our ex-Vice President challenged the Congress in the entire community college system. He went to Al Shanker, the president of the American Federation of Teachers (AFT) and obtained $25,000 to run a campaign against the Congress' leadership. He undoubtedly promised Shanker an affiliation with the AFT once the current leadership was ousted. An affiliation would have been attractive to Shanker because an affiliation means, among other things, that the parent union is entitled to a certain percentage of the affiliated members' dues. This percentage is referred to as per capitas or per caps.

Our ex-Vice President began to build an organization in the state, and he started speaking with different groups at several of the community colleges. I even debated him once at Manchester. Our counter-campaign was vigorous: our slogan was "organize the unorganized."

It was maddening to us that the representatives of the Board of Trustees did not stop our opponent from inappropriately using his college's resources to run his campaign. The Board had previously enforced with us a niggling clause in our contract that stipulated that 4 C's members were not authorized to use any college supplies, even stationery and memo pads, to conduct union business. After debating the issue internally, I decided to alert the Executive Director of the Board that our renegade former Vice President was running his campaign with company supplies on company time. To expose a member's inappropriate behavior to management could have opened the way for our ex-Vice President to file a DFR or Duty of Fair Representation lawsuit against us. A union is obligated by law to defend all of its members and to not knowingly expose them to potential disciplinary action.

Fortunately, or unfortunately, this particular member had bigger fish to fry. I should explain here that one of the banes of the labor movement is the frequency of raids of one union against another. At stake is which organization will represent the members. Under labor law at the national and state levels, there is by necessity a mechanism for changes in bargaining unit representation if workers are dissatisfied. That is why contracts of excessive duration are forbidden. In many cases, lengthy contracts have been dissolved by the appropriate labor board. Contracts of three, four, or even five years are the maximum allowed; the only time a raid can legitimately take place is when a union's contract has expired. The procedure for a change in representation is the same as for the initial designation of a bargaining unit. The raiding union must file collective bargaining cards signed by a minimum of 35% of the members, while those who file later, called "interveners" may submit cards signed by as few as 10% of the members.

Another form that jurisdictional disputes can take is when various unions compete for what tasks or responsibilities will be performed by which union members. This problem is particularly acute in the building trade unions, where a constant battle over jurisdiction goes on. For example, in the construction of a new high-rise in New York

City, the elevator for the workers on the outside of the building can be operated only by a member of the IBEW, the International Brotherhood of Electrical Workers— because it is run by electricity.

To return to the raid against us, our Achilles heel was an unfortunate error we had made earlier on, one about which our ex-Vice President had even warned us, but to no effect. This was that we had gone along with our attorney's suggestion to have our members' non-teaching duties more carefully spelled-out. In our faculty members' contracts, 80% of their work time was allotted for teaching duties, and 20% for "additional responsibilities." However, our attorney had advised that the contracts should say exactly what those additional responsibilities would entail. This turned out to be one of our more costly mistakes because management then used these criteria to accuse some of our members of not properly fulfilling their additional duties.

Our disgruntled former Vice-President capitalized on some of our members' dissatisfaction with this situation. In addition, some popular members of the union supported his efforts, and drew other followers in their wake. For about six months, this challenge went on, culminating in an election in 1983, overseen by the Connecticut State Labor Board. There were three choices as to who would be the bargaining agent for the community college system: the Congress (no change), the Congress-AFT, and no union. Although we won the vote, it was too close for comfort. As I recall, we won by only a 58% majority.

We were unaffiliated at that time, and the close vote shocked us into a recognition of possible continuing danger. We therefore shopped around for an affiliation with

an AFL-CIO union. Article Twenty of the AFL-CIO constitution forbids raids of one CIO affiliate against another.
This is an Article that is seriously enforced, as the AFL
understands that such raids would be costly to the membership and of no value to itself. If one AFL-CIO-affiliated
union were to win an election against another, the number of per capitas paid to the parent union would not
change.

The Congress ended up with a joint affiliation with the
American Association of University Professors (AAUP)
and with the National Union of Hospital and Health Care
Employees (also called District 1199) a package which I
had put together with the encouragement of our Executive Board. My rationale for affiliation with 1199, one of
the most radical unions of the AFL-CIO, was that not only
would they offer us protection against raids, but they also
represented one of the largest union memberships in the
state.

My rationale for our affiliation with the more conservative AAUP was that it was a prestigious organization respected by even those of our members who were not particularly pro-union. Some of these members had not liked
our previous association with AFSCME, perceiving it to be
a union of the working class. It is interesting to note that
even the staid AAUP had been forced into the fray when a
number of its chapters at state universities had been given
collective bargaining rights under revised state laws. At
private colleges, on the other hand, chapters of the AAUP
were having a hard time getting recognized at all. In its
landmark 1980 anti-labor ruling, National Labor Relations Board v. Yeshiva University, the U.S. Supreme Court
had upheld Yeshiva's assertions against its chapter of the

AAUP that Yeshiva's faculty should be classified as managers, rather then workers. After the Yeshiva ruling, many of the nation's larger colleges and universities withdrew recognition of their faculty unions. Alarmed that the courts might target public colleges and universities next, the 4 C's prepared materials to defend ourselves. It was not difficult to find many instances where faculty committees in our system had been overruled by management personnel.

During Yeshiva's long and bitter struggle prior to the Supreme Court decision, I had been in contact with some of their organizers, but they had rejected my advice. I had suggested that, for drama's sake, they put on their yarmulkes (prayer caps) and tallitim (prayer shawls), open the doors of the sacred ark, remove the Torah containing the laws of the Holy Bible, and march around the University in a picket line.

District 1199 was a different sort of union than the AAUP. It was a rough-and-tumble organization, representing oft-exploited workers in nursing homes and hospitals. 1199 thought of themselves as a union of class struggle. My concern in working with them—and something I emphasized in all my contacts with other unions and with management—was that I wanted to deal only with principals. I did not want people on the tenth floor in Manhattan (a reference for those in the know to the Communist Party headquarters) to be dictating our behavior. It was widely rumored that Jerry Brown, the leader of 1199 in New England, was a member of the Communist Party. As part of our affiliation talks with him, I told Jerry, "If you are a Communist, I have no problem with that; I think unions have a right to elect whomever they wish to lead them. But I want to deal directly with principals, and not with denizens of the tenth floor." Jerry assured me that he and his elected leaders were the only people with whom we would be working. I replied that if we ever discovered that this was not true, we would march out the door. Jerry and I had a friendly relationship ever after, cooperating closely on key legislative battles, and working together to get agreement from others on strengthening the contract language for all state employees.

Although the AAUP had also worked in tandem with us in the state legislature, our negotiating problems with them were dissimilar. Unfortunately, the AAUP had a firm belief that they were God's gift to higher education in the United States, and that the many publications of their members offered proof of their intellectual superiority. In our initial affiliation talks, AAUP representatives handed me a document which stated they wanted us to submit all of our new contract proposals to them for approval. Naturally, we would not agree to such a foolish requirement. I told them that they had the shoe on the wrong foot: we should be making that demand of them. They had recently formed an agreement with a number of American colleges to require compulsory retirement for college professors at age 65. This was their attempt to solve the problem of faculty job shortages. Along with hundreds of others across the country, my brother-in-law, an economics professor at Franklin and Marshall College, had been forced to retire at 65. The college had then turned around and hired him back as a part-time teacher at a much lower salary. There was no way that our members would have put up with such an unfair policy. In Connecticut, after a legal battle waged by the public school teachers' unions, a man who was 84 years old was allowed to continue teaching in high school.

In the context of affiliation, another observation could well be made. It illustrates a warning issued by Lord Acton, a British historian of the 19th century, "Power corrupts, and absolute power corrupts absolutely." Before we made our decision to affiliate, some members of the AFT local from the technical colleges approached me to suggest that we reconsider going with the AFT. I did not authorize them to negotiate for us with Shanker, but I did say that we had spent $25,000 defending ourselves against the attempted raid, and one condition for us even talking with the Shanker people was that the AFT must repay us for our loss. The AFT members, it turned out, did speak to Shanker, and he agreed that if we were to affiliate with them, they would give us a check for $25,000. As stated above, the AFT spent at least that much for their raid, so that meant they were willing to spend a total of $50,000 on affiliation with the Congress. What a way to waste the members' dollars!

CHAPTER

8

Extending Our Reach

T HE 1975 LEGISLATION AUTHORIZING COLLECTIVE BAR-
GAINING for state employees did not prescribe how
bargaining over retirement and health benefits
would take place. For a number of years, various unions
of Connecticut's workers bargained with the state individually for their own retirement and health benefits, often
duplicating each other's efforts. These negotiations were
thus a big time-waster for management and employees
alike.

About nine years after the original legislation was
passed, an amendment was added, establishing that state
employees could bargain over retirement and health
benefits if, and only if, they bargained as a single entity.
Unfortunately, this was easier said than done. Months after the amendment was passed, the different unions of
state employees were still not acting as a cohesive group.
I knew that state workers would get nowhere unless we
could work together, so, after consulting the 4 C's attorney, Don Pogue, I went ahead with a plan. I invited representatives of the twelve unions for dinner and drinks at an
Italian restaurant in downtown Hartford, ensuring high

attendance by telling them that the 4 C's would pick up the tab. I then explained to the gathered assemblage that, in the absence of any agreement on our part, the state could and probably would summarily make decisions for us. If we did not learn to work together—and quickly—we would be lose an opportunity to protect the interests of our constituents.

It was thus that SEBAC, the State Employees' Bargaining Agent Coalition, was born. To cool worries that one unit or a group of units could end up with greater power than the others, I used a technique that had helped me a few years earlier when I had helped organize a precursor to SEBAC, the Pension Coordinating Committee. At the heart of this technique was the idea that each unit could have one issue of their choice, no matter how large or small, that they could bring to arbitration with the state. To be sure that this idea would be understood at the meeting, I had explained it to several of the participants ahead of time, and had made sure that I would have the votes to put it through. The police officers had told me, before the meeting, that they wanted to have as their chosen issue retirement at any age, as long as their twenty-year minimum period of service had been met. The teachers, on the other hand, said they wanted their previous service in other school systems to be included in their seniority rankings and retirement benefits. Since each of the groups in the coalition would have one nonnegotiable issue, everyone felt secure that the playing field would be level. I also worked hard to ensure that any language we used was clear and unequivocal. To paraphrase an old saying, where there is a will, lawsuits are not required. As I write, SEBAC is still in business, and working together has become more or less habitual.

So, small unions can be effective beyond their size, if people in a small union spend some time thinking through what to do and how to do it. There are some labor leaders who are marvels at tactical arrangements, yet long-range strategic thinking often eludes them. Strategic thinking, however, is necessary for a union's success.

People often ask, where does this kind of thinking originate? It comes from considering problems, and how they can be resolved. Thinking this way also involves recognition of the desires and needs of others. Union members may sometimes regard new leaders with an element of distrust, but once a leader has demonstrated that he or she has their best interests at heart, they will work with the leader in a much more relaxed manner.

Einstein found time to think by getting a job in the Swiss patent office. Not to compare myself with his genius, but I found time to think by deliberately setting aside a few hours each week for a planning session with myself. At these planning sessions I asked myself, and answered truthfully, what was working, and what was not, and which goals had been reached, and which had not. If necessary, I would then find new and more realistic goals.

Strategic thinking, and a little intelligence-gathering, were necessary when Former U.S. Senator Lowell Weicker was elected Governor in 1990 with strong support from the unions, including the 4 C's. Faced with what appeared to be an ongoing problem of budget shortfalls, the Governor proposed severe budget cuts as soon as he took office, including cuts to the State Employees' and Teachers' Pension Funds. Fortunately, SEBAC and its allies were able to beat back the worst of Weicker's proposals.

The defeat of Mr. Weicker's first attempt on the state workers' retirement funds regrettably did not prevent him from trying, a few months later, to reduce the amount of money that state workers would receive in their pensions. As with many public pension funds, the state of Connecticut had not kept pace with its required yearly contributions. In a move that would have reduced the state's liability for pension contributions in the past, present, and future, Weicker decided to use a new method to calculate what the state owed its retirees. He decided to set up a study group to make the changes he had in mind. This advisory body was to be composed of one member appointed by the Governor, one by the Treasurer, one by the top dog in the state senate, and so forth. All of the appointments had been made, save one—a member to be named by the majority leader in the House of Representatives. The majority leader at that time was Representative Krawicki, a Democrat who was very conservative on financial issues.

By talking to various people in state government, I had been able to figure out that the advisory group would be split evenly down the middle on whether to approve the Governor's proposed recalculations. It was clear that whomever Krawicki appointed to the group would have the power to swing the vote in one direction or the other. I drafted a careful letter to Krawicki in which I pointed out that state workers would have less money on which to retire if the Governor's proposals went through. Though I knew that Krawicki and I were in the same pension fund, I did not state this fact, as I thought that would be bad form. I did ask him outright if he would appoint me to the new advisory group. I had a few people look over the letter before

I dispatched it to Kawikci, and then I awaited his reply. Lo, and behold, he appointed me to the group! The Weicker people proceeded to go ape. They had assumed Krawicki would be on their side, but they had never actually asked his opinions on the matter. They knew that I was a bull-dog on issues that affected our members, and that I had a reputation as a very convincing speaker. They never called a meeting of the new group.

The qualities of mind and soul necessary for being a U.S. Senator and the governor of a state are remarkably dissimilar. As a U.S. Senator, Weicker had

played the role of a knight in white armor, crusading for various idealistic causes. A governor, however, must focus on the nitty-gritty details of running a state. Weicker and his friends had presupposed that they would be able to get the votes for their point of view. They had forgotten the first rule of politics: you must have the ability to count.

CHAPTER
9

The Importance of Humor in
Union Work and in Life

"**L**AUGH AND THE WORLD LAUGHS WITH YOU: WEEP AND you weep alone." From time to time, my mother would repeat to me this wisdom from Ella Wheeler Wilcox's poem, "Solitude." It fit in with a conviction of mine that humor has a real place in life experience, whether one is selling shoes or selling the idea of a union.

In 1994, a number of the twelve SEBAC unions emerged from arbitration with a modest award not pleasing to state officials. The state then announced it wanted to renegotiate the contracts, a clear violation of the wording in our collective bargaining agreement that any arbitration would be "final and binding." SEBAC could have filed an unfair labor practice charge at that point, but, if we had done so, we would have been involved in a long drawn-out court case, and most likely would have ended up damaging some relationships with key management players. So we decided to renegotiate the contracts. Ironically, what we came away with was not all that different from the original contracts.

Perhaps a short detour into a discussion of arbitration

would be in order. Arbitration had proved to be a very powerful weapon for the union movement, and, whether or not they were willing to admit it, for management, as well. It was a means of resolving what often were very sensitive issues.

With arbitration, a neutral third party rules on the negotiations or disputes between two other parties, and the words final and binding have special significance. They mean that management cannot legally sneak out of an arbitrator's decision. Yet, there is also a legal hitch to the words final and binding. They clash headlong with another concept: the long-established precedent in English and American common law that is summed up by the phrase, "sovereign immunity." Sovereign immunity means that the sovereign, or, in this case, the state, cannot and will not give away its power to the upstart unions. The Connecticut state legislature had for many years thus maintained the right to review, and override, any labor arbitrator's decisions. Various members from the 4 C's had worked with the legislature, however, to soften the impact of sovereign immunity, and had created a new system in which a minimum of twelve votes by Senators could cancel out a legislative override of an arbitrator's award. This was a clever compromise which illustrates the old saying that a good agreement is one from which both parties walk away from the negotiating table a little dissatisfied.

Once an arbitrator had ruled on the unions' negotiations with the state, the process required that the funding of each union's individual contract be approved by the state Senate. In the 1995 legislative session, we knew that we had eleven Senators on whom we could count, but then some enterprising unionists convinced a Republican senator to change his vote, and we had arrived at the necessary number of twelve.

With the Senators in place, I knew that the contract for the 4 C's would pass, but I wanted us to get more than the minimum number of votes. I wanted to demonstrate that state unions were significant actors and that we had a future. Some of the other contracts from SEBAC had already passed, but I had not gleaned any clues from their passage on how to specially plead our case. I knew that I could not cite the additional support of the twelfth Senator since that might well lead to a GOP hunt to find the miscreant and spoil everything.

I usually did not appear before the legislature for the purpose of lobbying. But whenever the Congress submitted a contract, I always made a presentation. In my presentation that day, I stressed the dismay of our members over the stream of verbal attacks on our unions published in **The Hartford Courant**, the local anti-labor medium. I pointed out how hard our members worked, and that many of our students needed extra help to succeed in college. To be constantly demeaned in the media was very demoralizing. Our members would appreciate some support from the legislature, which a strong vote for our contract would signify.

The Chairman of the joint House and Senate appropriations committee, Bill Dyson, said in response to my pitch that he and the other legislators were also disappointed that many worthwhile ideas had not found sufficient support in the Legislature to be approved. The Representative said that he and the other members of the Legislature felt that they were equally unappreciated. Lightning struck: I had my "in."

I started to say, "To paraphrase the words of Karl Marx, unappreciated–" but I was cut off by Chairman Dyson,

who snapped, "What did you say?" He said this not out of
ill will, but undoubtedly because he was bored with all the
arguments presented to him each day: he wanted to stir
the pot a little to make his life more interesting.

Because so many unions were involved, every one of
the 200 chairs in the hall was occupied. I was sitting at a
small table just in front of the committee, which was on
a platform raised a few inches off the floor. I waited qui-
etly, a little smile hovering on my lips, since I wanted to
increase the tension in the room. I did not make the mistake of saying, "You interrupted me," or, worse yet, "Are
you trying to redbait me?" When I had the full attention
of every listener, I said, in a normal tone, "As I was saying, to paraphrase the words of Karl Marx, unappreciated
of the world unite." A tremendous burst of laughter ran
through the hall, and I was later told by a state legislator
that it was the biggest laugh of the legislative session.

Our contract passed handily. I did not know until just
a few weeks ago, when I talked to Dan Livingston about
it, that our union's contract was the only one out of the
twelve of SEBAC that was passed by a clear majority. This
occurrence demonstrates the importance of humor in
union work, as well as in life. Humor can not only relieve
tension in difficult situations, but it can also help make
friends and win people over.

As the laughter died down, and as I stood to return to
my seat, the Chairman asked, "Sid, where do I go to register for your course?" Responding in the same gracious
tone, I replied, "Bill, you don't have to register for my
course. Any time you have a few spare moments, please
feel free to drop in."

It was easy to be gracious in this case. A legislator could

visit my class on the basis of a simple invitation, but most academic teaching contracts stipulate that management personnel, such as a dean or a college president, can enter a faculty member's classroom only when certain requirements have been met.

Of course, my use of humor was not confined to collective bargaining situations. I had a large repertoire of jokes, some racy, others not, plus an ability to utilize humor in a variety of situations, including the classroom. I studied part-time for ten years to get a Master's Degree from Trinity College in Hartford. One year, I could not find a class at night which fit into my desired curriculum. I considered myself a Europeanist, but the only available class was in American colonial history. The professor, a Dr. Weaver, was an expert in that field, with a host of publications to his credit. The class met for three hours once per week. On the first night of class, it was customary for the professor to hand out a course outline, discuss the books on the reading list, and give a perfunctory lecture. A term paper was a required part of the course. I had never done a term paper at the University of Chicago, but I was not worried about it. One of my classmates, however, a young man in his twenties who worked for an insurance company, was puzzled. He asked Dr. Weaver to explain what a term paper was, but the professor was stumped. The best he could do was mutter, "You know, a term paper."

I was angered by our teacher's lack of response. We students were paying $750 per course, and the young man deserved an answer. The good professor went on with his lecture, using notes on yellowed sheets of paper that had once been white. He talked about the villages of the aborigines, now called Native Americans. Their villages, he said, consisted of a row of tents, with bare earth in between, and a full quota of barking dogs. One of the students in the class was a Miss Jane Cheney, the curator of the children's museum in the city where I lived. Full of excitement, she asked, "What kind of dogs were they?" The professor stood with his mouth open. Perhaps some anthropologist knew the answer, but I doubt it. The DNA of these dogs was probably a mystery. Springing manfully—or rather, personfully—into the gap, I clarified the situation, suggesting, sotto voce, "You know, dogs, just like term papers." Everyone laughed, including Dr. Weaver.

My reward for extricating him from a difficult position was a B in the course, despite the fact that he had told me that my term paper was worth publishing (which it wasn't). He knew that he could not go lower than a B without inspiring some retaliation from me. It so happened that I was not at all grade conscious, and, in any event, I was later informed by someone in the Dean of Student's Office that when I finished my ten courses at Trinity, I had achieved the highest Grade Point Average of any student in the Master's program there.

My lowered grade in Dr. Weaver's history class was worth it. Surprisingly for an historian, Dr. Weaver had neglected to pay proper attention to the facts. In the class was a student named Pauline who was the Dean of Faculty's private secretary. She and I had a good laugh when we discussed Dr. Weaver's shortcomings over a cup of coffee. I did not ask her to do anything. I did not have to. The following semester, the course in American colonial history that Dr. Weaver had taught for years was taken away from him, and he was given an entirely different course which required a new preparation. *Noli me tangere.*

CHAPTER
10

Personality and Collective Bargaining

MANY PERSONALITY TYPES CAN BE SUCCESSFUL IN COL-
LECTIVE bargaining: shouters, tough guys and
gals, manipulators, and more. I preferred a
rational approach, although this approach does require
some rationality on the part of the other side. We had
always used our attorney in arbitrations, but, finally, a few
years before I retired, I tried my hand at representing our
interests. The arbitrator was Tim Bornstein, a well-known
arbitrator who occasionally wrote about the art of arbitration. When I had finished presenting my first case, he
said, "You did well, and with your usual grace." Both parts
of his compliment pleased me, but the remark about
"grace" pleased me more, since my goal was to act with
grace in whatever I did. I could yell with the best of them,
but I rarely resorted to that technique.

Bob Vater had been a yeller, and, as his aide, I had never tried to change him. The difference in our styles had
been evident in our negotiations with Alan Drachman,
who was often employed as a management defender by
various educational organizations. Very early on in an exchange between Bob and Alan, Bob threatened that the

Congress would go on strike. He did so without consulting either the other leaders or the members as to their willingness to take such an action. Drachman snapped back, "You don't have the balls." Vater fell silent, but I replied, "No, but we do have the ovaries." I was referring to the fact that three of the eight members of our bargaining team were women, while management had no females on their negotiating team at all. I noticed that, by the next session, management had been able to find some women for their side. In any case, Vater was very precipitous in his threat to go on strike without checking with anyone first.

Drachman had a wealth of experience in negotiations with the American Federation of Teachers local for the Boston schoolteachers, and in many cases, their negotiating style was very similar to Bob's. Drachman knew how to deal with that style before he walked in the door. Bob's blustering was therefore ineffectual with Drachman.

I must hurry to point out, however, that the shouters and the blusterers often won victories in collective bargaining by adapting their personal styles to the scenarios that confronted them. All of the methods I discuss here can be jiggled and juggled in various life situations. Swimming in the dangerous waters of conflict demands a cool head and an active mind.

The Board of Trustees' representatives were cognizant of my style. This was evident at the retirement party for Walter Markiewicz, who was Dean of the College at Greater Hartford Community College, and who was second in line to the President in his school's hierarchy. I was invited to his retirement luncheon, but could not attend, since I had a speaking engagement in North Carolina. I asked the Congress' number one staffer, Sonia Berke, if she could go in my place. She returned with the following report. When Markiewicz responded to a variety of laudatory comments, he said, "Everything I know about collective bargaining, I learned from Sid and Sonia." This was an exaggeration, but Markiewicz was angry, since the Executive Director of the Board of Trustees had promised him a college presidency many times, but had never followed through. His comment must have been embarrassing to Jack Foley, who was present at the luncheon. Continuing in the same vein, Markiewicz said, "Lipshires' word is as good as his bond." That much was certainly true.

Recognition is always sweet, but I was more interested in getting the job done than in being recognized. My members recognized the results, and that was enough for me. Still, after I had retired, it was very meaningful to me when students, union members, or former colleagues would thank me for my work. A dramatic case in point was when I had to be rushed to the hospital one night because a pain medicine I was taking had caused my stomach to leak two pints of blood. As I was being wheeled into the emergency room, a familiar face appeared by my gurney, and a loud voice boomed out, "Here is the guy who taught me everything I know about collective bargaining." The voice belonged to Carmine Centrella, the president of the Protective Services union, one of the original SEBAC member unions. His words of praise, though appreciated, were not quite true. Carmine had already known the most important thing about collective bargaining, and that was on which side of the table he was supposed to sit.

In my view, Jack Foley never grasped all of the essentials of collective bargaining. In contract negotiations, one naturally strives to win, but day-to-day contract administration, on the other hand, should be a process of resolving problems. Jack told me one time that he saw contract administration as being like a hockey game: Jack's pursuit of victory in these circumstances missed the point. A good contract administrator will always look for ways to compromise and fulfill the terms of the agreed-upon contract.

In our long, drawn-out contract disputes with Jack, we generally ended up with something very close to the first settlement offer we had made. This meant that even when Jack conceded something, he really got no credit for having settled because people were so soured by his delays. I had learned some valuable lessons about how to correctly handle disputes by observing my father in his retail shoe store. When a customer came in with a complaint, he always asked the customer to sit down, and perched himself on a fitting stool. He then listened intently to the complaint, and, when he offered a settlement, he did so with a smile.

A facility with languages is an asset in almost any situation involving negotiations and bargaining. American English is my native tongue. French is my second language (part of my World War II service was as an interpreter in France), Yiddish is my third, and I can at least order a meal and get a hotel room in both Italian and German.

It is not necessary to be able to speak a foreign language, however, to excel at collective bargaining. The main requirement is that one be able to speak the ever-changing language of give-and-take. This means that one must stay alert for sudden changes in the emotional atmosphere, and must be ready to improvise when the unexpected occurs.

CHAPTER
11

Negotiating Techniques and Problems

I THINK THAT NEGOTIATING CAN BE LEARNED FROM PARTICI-
PATION and observation, and also by following some
pointers from people who are experienced in the
field. For those who are approaching union negotiations
for the first time, it is important not to allow oneself to become intimidated by the mystique of negotiating. Some
people believe that only lawyers know how to negotiate
well. This is not true. Law schools do not generally teach
negotiating skills. Some lawyers are naturally very good at
negotiating, while others are not good at it at all.

How do you learn to negotiate? You begin by negotiating with the people who have the most power in your
life—your parents. If bedtime is at 9:00, and if you are a
halfway decent negotiator, you can squeeze out an extra
five or ten minutes to watch an entertaining show on tele-
vision. You know enough not to say, "I'm not going to bed
now, and you can't make me." After you learn to negotiate with your parents, you go on to negotiate with your
siblings, schoolmates, teachers, teammates, and so on.

In union negotiations, it is very important to take the
time to know what you are doing. Before you approach

the negotiating table, make sure you thoroughly understand and make explicit to yourself your goals. Be sure that all of the members of your negotiating team have the same understanding of your shared objectives.

In a special session with your team, go over the demands submitted by both sides, and answer everyone's questions. Be sure your team realizes how important this process is. Then give the following instructions: all team members can speak during negotiations, but whatever they say when management is in the room must support the union's positions. Your team must understand that you, as the chief spokesperson, will be the only member designated to make proposals to management. Tell the team that if any of them has a question about what you are saying at the negotiating table, they can pass a note to you requesting a caucus. You, of course, will comply with any such requests. If there is not a good fit between you and your team, or among your team members, they either have been wrongly chosen or wrongly instructed.

Make their responsibilities clear to your team members. Since you yourself will be seated directly opposite the other side's designated negotiator, your gaze will be directed at that person. Your team members must therefore constantly watch the other side's silent members to gauge their reactions to your proposals. Ask your team members to observe and take notes on when the others nod their heads, frown, smile, or whatever. These notes should be provided to the entire team at the next opportunity.

When your team members observe emotional clues on the management side, use this information to your best advantage. Someone who laughs or nods their head in agreement with your points may represent a chink in the armor of the other team. If one of your team members knows someone on the management side, by all means encourage that member to privately engage the person in conversation. It's best if your team member starts off by talking about non-controversial topics before moving on to the subject of the negotiations. The point is to break up the solidarity of your opponents.

Comport yourself in the negotiations with seriousness, but do not be stuffy. Speak in a calm voice and display a relaxed manner. Why should you not be relaxed? You know that in the end your side will succeed. Do not be a wise guy, however. Explain your proposals completely, but do not wear your heart on your sleeve. Whether you hear good news or bad, show no emotion. As our attorney Don Pogue suggested to us, attempt to deal with each problem clinically—in other words, with detachment. You will do better with this approach. Pretend you have been hired to do a job, and go ahead and do it.

You are legally obligated to deal seriously with any proposals from the other side. Make sure that you do so. Failing to discuss demands that you think are foolish will not carry the day. If their proposals are not clear, ask questions until you are certain you understand them. Other things being equal, take care not to insult your opponents. Demonstrate how your proposal not only suits your needs, but also takes into consideration the needs of management and your students. Even when you know you will never go along with a particular demand, act like you are taking it into consideration. Say, "We'll think about it," or something similar.

One thing to guard against is negotiating fatigue. For

our first contract with the Board of Trustees, we spent around 14 months in meetings before we got a settlement. This was very frustrating. During this time period, Bob Vater and I attended an AFSCME convention where we met a group of people from the Midwest with whom we discussed our long, drawn-out negotiations. They told us that first contracts always take a lot of time, and advised us to just hang in there. They said that the same thing had happened to them, but that one day the management negotiators walked in and said, "Do you want a contract? Let's settle today." So they did.

Negotiating fatigue is similar to a kind of fatigue that sometimes besets Wall Street investors. Investors can get weary of assessing the constant fluctuations of the market. They get tired of hearing about the market, of reading about it, and of watching its gyrations. They begin to feel they can no longer take the uncertainty, so they precipitously sell their stocks. Later, when they cool down, they may realize that they had made a mistake.

Negotiators, tiring of the lengthy process, may also give away their own best interests. The chief negotiator should stay alert to this possibility, and pay attention to what his or her team members are saying. Are members of your team saying that they are feeling tired, restless, or frustrated? Don't allow yourself to become so preoccupied with how the negotiations are going that you lose sight of these vital signs. It could be that one of your team members has to miss an important date because he is tied up in negotiations, or perhaps the wife of another team member gets annoyed because her husband no longer participates fully in caring for their children. To prevent frustrated team members from throwing in the towel, periodically give people a few days away from the negotiating table. I was also careful not to schedule any negotiating sessions on any team member's birthday or anniversary.

One of the benefits of being on our negotiating team was the pleasant dinners we occasionally scheduled for ourselves after the day's sessions were over. We wouldn't go to the most expensive places, but we would find restaurants that served good food. It was a pleasant way to unwind, and the dinners helped us fight burn-out and fatigue. The Board of Trustees did not offer to pay for nice meals for their own negotiators. They had to dine at inexpensive chain restaurants. The question is, what kind of negotiators were they if they couldn't even negotiate a decent dinner for themselves? I would rather bargain with people who could negotiate well for themselves, because they would be more likely to understand our needs.

Usually, in any negotiation, the union's chief negotiator will ask his counterpart on the management side if he or she is authorized to settle the issues at hand. Of course, the answer is always yes. Occasionally, however, after a settlement is presumably reached, the management representative will return for a private talk with his counterpart to report, with considerable chagrin, "I have some bad news: I could not sell this agreement to my principals. Could you let me off the hook?" If this is an infrequent request, you should give the person a break. Why? Because the same thing could possibly happen to you. However, if this happens too often, you have a real problem on your hands. What is the point of going through negotiations if you are uncertain of the outcome, and, in a very real sense, may have to start over?

On the union side, the best way to handle a repeat offense of this kind is to demand a meeting with the principals who have the power to make decisions. Naturally, there is plenty of room for drama here, including some yelling. The union could refuse to negotiate until a remedy to this problem is found. The option of last resort is to file an unfair labor practice charge with the appropriate labor board.

There are some dangers in filing such a charge. The longer negotiations are delayed, the more likely it becomes that the employer, in this case the State of Connecticut, could declare an impasse, and make decisions for the two parties without prior notice. An additional worry for management when a union files such charges is that if the labor board confirms the charges, the loser will be covered with ignominy. This outcome could well lead to other unions insisting on stronger authorizations to settle from the same management group before negotiations can even begin.

Other complications could interfere with a clear run to a settlement. A friend in another union consulted me one time about a local school board that had charged a male high school science teacher with making a sexist remark. He had been trying to get a duplicator to work in a classroom filled with students, and when he had trouble with the machine, he said with exasperation, "This machine must be a female, it's so difficult to deal with." Several of the students reported the incident to their parents, who complained to the school board. This case ended up in arbitration. In the course of his presentation to the arbitrator, the school board's representative exclaimed, "Not only do we have this problem at hand, but we also have had a long string of other complaints against this same teacher over the years." The teacher's union contract stated that in this type of situation, the school board would be required to list all of the complaints against the teacher and to discuss each of them individually, none of which the school board had done.

The representative handling this case for the union failed to follow up on the school board's lack of documentation, and was at a loss for what to do. If I had been representing the union in this dispute, I would have seized the opportunity for a little drama. First, I would have asked our note-taker (each side had one) to read back the last few sentences from his or her notes. Following that reading, I would have asked my counterpart on the other side to step out into the hall for a private discussion. I would then have pointed out the great defect in his charges, and would have suggested in strong terms that he was going to come out the loser in this case.

Next, I would have suggested a different resolution. We could agree on a mild reprimand for the teacher and to put an end to the arbitration. There would have been the possibility of some valuable assistance from the arbitrator at this point, in a private discussion with both parties. If handled correctly, not only would the union have prevailed, but the management representative would have seriously lost face, including with his employer. If the union's reps were professionals, there could have been an outcome of this kind. Amateurs, though strongly committed to their cause, would not have known what to do or how to do it.

The 4 C's eventually developed a successful negotiating strategy that we used each time a contract was renewed, but I don't know if the Board's team ever caught on. We would handle the matter in the following fashion. We would meet with the Board's negotiating team, and focus on the easy issues first, settling those matters on which both sides could readily agree. We would next push for those issues that meant the most to our union, spending whatever time was necessary to reach an agreement. We then would turn our attention to the issues that we knew were of concern to management only. Since it would have been an unfair labor practice not to touch on every proposal, we would at least mention every item, sometimes saying in a disarmingly friendly fashion, "Well, you know, we're not going to agree to that one." Then, when the patience of the Board's representatives began to wear thin, we would suggest that we had settled all the tough issues we were going to agree upon, and that we all should just wrap things up. I would hurry the process along by saying that I had some bottles of high-quality champagne waiting in the refrigerator as a reward for our completed negotiations. This method always seemed to work, so I can state with confidence that both prioritizing one's issues and offering a good champagne are important weapons in any negotiating team's arsenal.

Another important weapon is a good understanding of psychology. I used to tell my colleagues in the Psychology Department at Manchester that I had had only one course in psychology in college, but that I had learned everything I knew about general psychology from selling women's high-fashion shoes. This was at least 98% true. My knowledge came in handy when dealing with irate students, or members, and also with those who sat across from me in negotiations. My knowledge of Freud which I used in writing my doctoral dissertation came in handy, too, especially since I had learned from my study of Marx not to worship any of the great thinkers uncritically.

In talking to psychoanalysts, I had often remarked that I was one of the few people in the country who had read all of Freud's collected works, which consisted of 19 volumes, not counting the index. In a jocular mood, I would sometimes say that because the German language tends to leave the verbs at the end of a sentence, all of the verbs in Freud's works were in the last volume.

More seriously, my readings in Freud provided me with considerable insights into the unconscious workings of the human mind. These insights were helpful in understanding some of the more curious attitudes of the people sitting across from me in negotiations. I learned too, from my readings, to come to the negotiating room early enough to grab the seats in the shade, while our opponents would have to content themselves with sitting in the sunlight where we could observe them more closely.

We had two main problems dealing with the Board of Trustees. The first was the community college presidents. I cannot recall any point in our history when there were more than three good college presidents out of the twelve in the system. If the three were given their head, we would have had no problem settling local grievances, and not always because they were willing to give away the store. We could have worked well with those presidents because they, like us, regarded themselves as advocates for the community college system. However, these presidents were not allowed to settle when they would have chosen to because Jack Foley always said, "No."

To be fair, Jack's job really should have been divided among two or three people. I had said this to him and to two different Executive Directors of the Board a number of times. Jack was, in essence, the Board's attorney, their contract negotiator and administrator, and also their personnel director—an impossible mix of responsibilities. Jack's job was to represent the interests of the employer, but one of those interests should have been to assure that the employees were treated with consistency and fairness.

Jack faced the added difficulty of working with a Board that was divided from within. Although the Board's meetings were confidential, as were ours, we had heard snippets of information which indicated that the Board harbored two members who were fervidly anti-union, and one person who was moderately so. The Executive Board of the 4 C's was almost always unanimous in its decisions, but Jack had the misfortune of serving a variety of masters who were not always in agreement.

I was pleased to observe that, after about seven years of an antagonistic relationship with the 4 C's, Jack began to modify his behavior to some extent. I think he began to realize that we were not a danger to his job or to the community college system about which he genuinely cared. Jack and the Board even tried sometimes to take credit with the state legislature for positive things we had done to advance the system's interests.

I, too, mellowed a bit, over time. It was interesting to note, however, that while I mellowed, our members became more militant. I think this militancy came about as a reaction to bad leadership in management. I lost count of the number of times that members who had participated elsewhere in collective bargaining would ask me how I could stand it. My usual reply was an old one: "I don't care what people call me, as long as they don't call me late for dinner." My interest was always in resolving problems, and getting management to view us as the education-positive people we were. Any time I needed to blow off steam, I could do it in my own house, where I could yell to myself as loudly as I wanted.

The representatives of the Board were not very popular with the legislature. Personally, I wouldn't have hired many of these people to work for me, especially not as public relations representatives. The Board of Trustees did not understand that the faculty and professional staff were an asset to their system, not a liability. Some of the members of the Board may also not have understood what the community colleges could have done for the state of Connecticut. Imaginative leadership could have used the community colleges, for example, to develop a plan to combat what is known as "structural unemployment" (the kind that doesn't go away because it is caused largely by unemployability). Because of their lack of vision, the Board often worked against us, rather than with us. Such a negative relationship might pass muster in some venues, but not in one like ours where our members were the only real producers. Our members were also deeply rooted in the communities in which they lived, and had a long history of dealing with problems with the state. They were much better known to the state legislators than were the Board's representatives.

I didn't spend too much time bemoaning this situation, however, since I was too busy trying to handle it. I had to play the hand that I had been dealt.

CHAPTER
12

Creative Solutions to Money Issues

I THINK MOST PEOPLE WOULD AGREE THAT ONE OF THE MAIN purposes of a union is to help its members make economic gains. Our members had placed in us their trust that we would use their membership dues wisely to advocate for better wages and benefit packages for them. The leadership of the 4 C's took this trust very seriously, and, over the years, developed a number of solutions to the financial issues that most unions face. Some of these solutions we borrowed from other unions, but others I came up with myself. My solutions were creative not only because they resolved some of our problems, but also because they opened the door for management to come to terms with us.

One of the basic questions unions must decide is how membership dues will be calculated. It was common for many unions, such as District 1199, for example, to come up with a dues amount that they felt was necessary and fair, and then to campaign vigorously for an approving vote by the membership. After I became president of the 4 C's, we reevaluated our method for deciding on the amount of our dues. We felt that a periodic campaign over membership dues was a waste of the union's limited resources and time. Accordingly, with the members' approval, we set our dues at 1% of each member's wages. If wages went up through an increment or a better wage package, then 1% of the increased salaries would mean increased dues for the union.

Another challenge that all unions face is how to make financial settlements with management when both sides are reluctant to spend any money. By the end of my second term in office, I realized that one of the biggest obstacles to settling grievances was the lack of funding for that purpose. I therefore came up with the idea that, every year, one tenth of 1% of any wage packages we received through contract negotiations would go into an account we would call the Grievance Fund. Both the union and management would have to agree, on a case-by-case basis, upon the amount that could be drawn from this fund, but the fact that the fund existed made the financial settlement of grievances much more likely and swift.

As you might expect, we had in the 4 C's our share of ideologues, masochists, and nuts who commanded too much of our attention, but we knew—as did they—that we would always help them with their grievances. When some of these characters finally got tired of always being a problem to the boss, we would say to them, "Of course, we will defend you as long as you wish, but it's clear that management is never going to leave you alone. Have you ever considered retiring early?" If their answer was "yes," I had what I called a "Lipshires' Package" to offer them. It went like this: you leave and you get $9,000 cash, and, if you have a lot of time in, you also will get about $1200 more per year in retirement money. In addition, the boss will clean up your personnel file, and see that you get a letter of recommendation (which both of us would review in advance) or perhaps a promotion, if you missed out on one over the years. The Lipshires Package did not allow chiseling on either side. No, you could not get $9,100 in cash, and management could not get away with offering you only $8,900. Some of the money for these settlements, by agreement between the parties, could come from the Grievance Fund.

We would tell the grievant that the offer was non-negotiable, and we would tell management the same thing. After a while, the exact nature of the settlement would be set in the two parties' minds, and off we would go. If I had a problem with management's response to the offer, I would gather up my papers, throw them into my briefcase, and say politely, but firmly, "The offer just expired 10 minutes ago. I had a lot of trouble dealing with the grievant on this issue, so it's possible that we might be back six months from now. The ball is in your court." I would then walk away.

The fact that I was fortunate enough to possess numeracy as well as literacy was very helpful in my union work. This meant that I could easily penetrate the dark forest of numbers, and knew how to put them together. I could do quick math in my head at the bargaining table, and I thus stayed abreast of any discussions concerning money. My numeracy helped us achieve my goal of realizing a profit on every financial transaction the 4 C's took on, such as selling tickets to a memorial banquet. How do you think we accumulated a million dollar kitty during my years as president? I had a reputation for being a pinko, if not a red, so Sonia Berke took great delight in labeling me as the quintessential bourgeois. My reply was to look at our bank account balance and smile secretly to myself.

Once the state legally permitted pension issues to be included in collective bargaining, I studied the available literature about pension funds and familiarized myself with the language so that I would be well-equipped to assist our members. Because we negotiated for many different classes of employees across the state—police and counselors, teachers and registrars—I had to learn the different pension needs and rules governing each group. I also had to equip myself to answer our members' questions on whether it was better to belong to the teachers' or to the state employees' pension fund, what were the plusses and minuses of each plan, and how to move back and forth between the two systems. I was able to steer many of our members into taking out additional annuities, a highly advantageous investment since all of the money that was put into their annuities with TIAA-CREF (Teachers Insurance and Annuity Association-College Retirement Equities Fund) or into other retirement annuities was tax-free. This meant that these annuities would accumulate more rapidly, and taxes would only have to be paid on the money that was taken out—presumably, when a person's income was lower, after retirement. In fact, I always said that these pre-tax annuities were one of the best investments available to teaching professionals. I put my money where my mouth was and socked away as much money as I could into my own retirement annuity. I have been enjoying the benefits of that decision for many years now.

There were a few union members and personnel within the State Retirement System who knew as much or more than I did about retirement planning, and we made good use of their knowledge. Over the years, the Congress periodically invited these experts to speak to gatherings of our members and to answer their questions. We also enjoyed the good advice of the people at the headquarters of TIAA-CREF in New York City. I did not need to pay as much attention to issues around health insurance benefits, since our second labor attorney, Dan Livingston, was an excellent source of advice in this area.

In 1987, one of my best financial ideas was to establish a twenty-year minimum, which provided a minimum salary for those who had worked in the community college system for twenty years. I got the idea after preparing a scattergram of the salary range in the system. I could see that a minimum would provide a method for overcoming salary differences among those who had put in an equal amount of time. Its purpose would be to even out wage differences for people who had suffered unequal treatment because of conflicts with management or because of some other type of discrimination—usually based on gender or color. I myself had suffered from anti-union discrimination by not being promoted one year, although one year's delay did not affect me too grievously.

It must have been a sixth sense that prevented me from figuring out the entire cost of this plan for management, although the dollars for implementing it would have to come from a negotiated wage package in a given year. Thus, when I was asked, "What will the cost be?" I could honestly say, "I don't know."

It turned out that the value of the twenty-year minimum was so great that our members were 100% opposed to ever making a change to it. The only other issue that was untouchable in that way was the weekly twelve-credit-hour teaching load. At most other junior and community colleges in the nation, the standard teaching load had increased to fifteen hours per week. We often had to make compromises during our months-long negotiations with management, but, for us, the twenty-year minimum and the twelve-hour teaching load were sacrosanct.

The case of Tony Burns, who taught accounting at Middlesex Community College, and who also served as the treasurer for the 4 C's, illustrates the importance of the twenty-year minimum. For years, the president of Middlesex had engaged Tony in running battles over various policies. This president was intolerant of any questioning of his decisions. As a result, Tony had not received the promotions he had deserved. There had never been any dispute over his ability to teach, or over the respect with which he was held by dozens of students.

Early in our union's history, Tony and I, Jack Foley, the President of Middlesex, and a few other people from the union and management, had been assigned the task of deciding how a total of $75,000 in annual income would be divided among the 4 C's ACL (Administrators, Counselors, and Librarians) members. We came up with some guidelines for distributing this income, and then presented to the Board of Trustees a list of around 35 people who fit the guidelines. When the President of Middlesex saw that Tony's name was among those on the list, he went to the Executive Director of the Board of Trustees, and said that if Tony were included, he would not sign off on the Board's decision. The Executive Director then informed Jack Foley of this reality, and told Jack that Tony's name would have to come off the list. Jack was aware that this would have constituted an unfair labor practice dispute which we, of course, would have won. I told Tony that I would fight vigorously for his inclusion, but he demurred, saying that he didn't want the other people to be denied their money. I thought that Tony's stance was admirable: not many people would have sacrificed themselves in that way.

Some years later, Tony put in for an unusual two-jump promotion from Assistant Professor to Full Professor. Jack Foley asked me why he should agree to such a large increase, and I reminded him of how Tony had been cheated out of the other pot of money. Foley undoubtedly knew that what had happened to Tony was wrong, so he allowed Tony the two-step promotion. Months later, when Tony's promotion went through, the twenty-year minimum had been established. With his new rank, and with the new minimum in effect, Tony received an increase in salary of over $7,000 per year. Because each year the percentage of his raises would be based on his new higher salary, the total increase in his remuneration would be considerable over time.

When Jack saw how large Tony's increase was going to be, he blew a gasket. I said, as calmly as I could, "If you had a belief that strong, why did you agree to the twenty-year minimum?" It was clear that no one in management had actually computed the cost of the twenty-year minimum before they agreed to it.

Differences in wages among members of the same unit is one of the most volatile, and possibly divisive, issues that a union can face. Because there was such a discrepancy between the salaries of the highest and lowest paid workers in our unit, salary increases based on a percentage of salary would benefit the higher-paid workers more, while across-the-board increases would be of greater advantage to the lower-paid workers. To even out the benefits to employees on either end of the wage scale, we used a combination of percentage increases and across-the-board payments when negotiating our contracts. We were aware, however, that wage increases over time had created a group of workers who made $50,000 per year or more. We knew that, in order to keep the peace in our union, we would eventually have to put a cap on the highest salaries. We were not hesitant to do so, but just had not yet reached that point in our history. In any event, it was our goal to raise the lower paid workers' salaries at a faster rate in order to reduce the salary gap. We knew that if we narrowed that gap, there would be less danger that the dissatisfied lower paid workers would split away to form their own union or else make themselves available to work as scabs.

Juggling and adjustments have occurred at many unions where there are workers at opposite ends of the wage scale. In the auto industry, for example, the most highly paid workers were the tool and die makers. The work of the tool and die makers demanded a great deal more knowledge and skill than, say, assembling a new automobile from new parts. The unions that recognized this skill difference achieved a great deal more internal harmony than those that did not. Failure to reward greater skill with higher pay would often cause such a rift that the higher paid workers would split off from the original union and look to a new election to meet their needs.

Keeping a unit together is very much like preserving a marriage: unless various adjustments are made, the union can be lost. One could say with some degree of accuracy that a mediator can play a role similar to that of a marriage counselor in this connection. The leaders of a union must be helped to understand and be responsive to all of the possible threats to unity.

In the early 1980's, the issue of equal pay for comparable work (instead of the older slogan, equal pay for equal work) was one that could have threatened our unity if we had not addressed it head-on. Parity of benefits and pay between male and female employees had long been established among faculty at various institutions, but other professions had yet to reach that level of equality. Change was in the air, and when I realized we needed to reclassify the positions of our non-teaching colleagues (workers such as librarians, counselors, and administrators in various offices on our campuses) we felt the need to ask for outside, neutral help. We selected the well-recommended consulting firm of Norman D. Willis & Associates, partly because they had a national reputation for understanding how inequality in the workplace had kept women's salaries unfairly low. We were very satisfied with the results provided us by Willis & Associates, especially because management had no problem accepting their decisions. The community college system continues to use the Willis group's assistance with job reclassification to this day.

In the process of preparing for and working with the Willis group, we had to educate ourselves on how to assess and describe the tasks involved in many jobs. Probably the most difficult part of this process for our members was filling out a questionnaire asking them to break down what they did on the job. The question that stumped the most people was, "What is the most difficult part of your job?" It was always surprising to Sonia and me that so many people were incapable of scrutinizing their jobs with detachment. They were willing participants, but they lacked the analytic ability to answer this question meaningfully.

For example, one man who was an audiovisual director performed a variety of tasks, including lending machines to faculty, repairing machines, sending them out to be repaired, and so forth. His answer to the question about the most difficult part of his job was to say, "I have such a multitude of tasks to perform that I find it difficult to find time for them all."

One could correctly say that clerks who worked in a division office had to struggle with the same problem, but, in terms of comparable worth, his answer would not have netted him a salary increase. It wasn't the large amount of work that could give him a raise: we had to show that he was doing a different, more demanding type of work than others who were being paid at his level. I spent some time with him, and, in the course of our conversation, he informed me that he helped many teachers at his college develop training videos for their classes. I intuitively knew that he should say that this was the most difficult part of his job, but, just to be sure, I talked with my younger son, who was a filmmaker at that time and who developed audiovisual programs for various companies. My son assured me that making videos for training purposes was a highly creative function demanding special skills. Sonia and I had a devil of a time trying to convince our audiovisual director that this should be his answer, but he finally gave in. His position did not get recognized for an increase in the first round of analysis by the Willis group, but made it in the next one.

Another salary-related issue which we found necessary

to address was the hazardous nature of some peoples' jobs. For example, we had a counselor at Manchester who contacted us because he was concerned for his safety in the workplace. The counselors in our system handled a wide range of tasks, including academic advising and short-term psychological counseling. The counselor in question had told a particular student that, unfortunately, the student did not qualify for any sort of financial aid. The disgruntled student had returned the next day, and had pulled a four-foot length of axle spring from under his coat. He had laid the axle spring on the counselor's desk, and referred to it as a means of solving a variety of problems.

This story was very effective in our negotiations for a one-step increase in the labor grade for counselors at every school. But this increase then upset the age-old parity between librarians and counselors who, in our system, had always been at the same pay level. Jockeying such as this for what constitutes the most hazardous duty is common in municipal employment, where police and firefighters often compete for this designation. The librarians in our system were not happy about the change, but there was nothing we could do. At Harvard or some other elite four-year school, it was conceivable that a student might threaten a librarian who had not been able to procure a much-desired book, but, in our community colleges, the students did not seem to view books as necessities for their survival. I had about one hundred books on my shelves in my office at Manchester, and my door was never locked. No book was ever stolen. I would have felt better if it had been.

CHAPTER
13

Grievances and Beyond

S OME OF THE FOLLOWING MAY SEEM OBSCURE TO NON-PRAC-TITIONERS of the art of handling grievances, but I am trying to give my readers a real picture of the work of this union president. I have no statistical studies upon which to draw, but I can say with probable accuracy that we won a higher percentage of our grievances, and the arbitrations to which some of them led, than did most other unions.

I do know that we never lost a dismissal case during the eighteen years I was President of the 4 C's. We worked very hard on our grievances, but this does not fully explain our success. Some of the people whose cases we won should have been fired. But that was not our concern. We played a role similar to that of defense attorneys. We were obligated under labor law to represent any member who asked for our help, and we did. In addition, we held ourselves to very high standards of performance. We won even the less defensible cases because much of management was so remiss in their behavior. In my not-so-humble view, much of the top management in our system was made up of time-servers and incompetents. They were afraid that we would go public with what we knew about their faults of omission and commission.

For example, a former president of South Central Community College had repeatedly objected to how his business manager, a 4 C's member, prepared his yearly financial reports. The president had often pressured this man to change his methodology, even though the business manager was conforming to federal guidelines. It would have been better for employee and employer alike if the business manager had come to the 4 C's to tell us about this conflict earlier. We could have mediated the situation had we known about it then, but we did not hear of the problem until it came to a head.

One morning, the business manager had been having an argument with his wife on the way to work, and answered an early telephone call at his office, mistakenly thinking it was her. His angry expletive when he picked up the phone upset the community member who had called to ask an innocent question. The offended party complained to the college president, who seized upon this inappropriate behavior as an opportunity to oust the business manager. By proving that the president had been placing unwarranted pressure on the business manager all along, the 4 C's was able to downgrade his dismissal to a letter of discipline. We were also able to effectuate his transfer to a different community college where the president was delighted to find someone who understood the federal regulations so well.

Being well-informed about management's incompetence often allowed me to say to Jackson Foley, "I hate to bring discredit to our system, but you leave me no alternative." With the ace of good information up our sleeves, the

4 C's was able to downgrade many a move for dismissal to a much lesser form of discipline. It wasn't uncommon at our grievance hearings for us to hammer out agreements of this kind long into the night.

Mind you, not all the members of management were up to no good. At any given moment in our union's history, there were always those three college presidents with whom we could negotiate reasonably on local issues. In addition, a number of the various colleges' deans shared our beliefs in bettering the community college system. Even at the central office of the Board of Trustees, there were some personnel who clearly had the best interests of the workers and the students at heart. In addition, a number of other people who worked in support positions for management were deeply committed to the mission of the community colleges. We enjoyed working with them, and appreciated their hard work.

In our grievance hearings, we protected ourselves with some very good advice from our first attorney, Donald Pogue. He told Sonia and me—and we told the rest of the Congress' staff—that every grievance should be written as if the dispute would end in arbitration. In keeping with that advice, we invested a great deal of time and effort in the investigation and the writing of each grievance.

Another factor in our favor was our large reserve of ready cash. We sent our financial reports to our members, and we knew that someone in the union would always run to management with the reports, just to curry favor. Toward the end of my presidency, we had over one million dollars in assets, and thus had the ability to mount a very strong defense. We knew that knowledge of our assets often caused management to stop and consider our offers to settle. What would it have profited them to fight over every issue to the death?

Every time our union representatives went out to hold a grievance hearing, I always made a point to tell them what our bottom line was for a settlement. I also instructed them that if they discovered in the course of the hearing that our case was not as good as we had imagined, they should call me for advice before attempting to change that bottom line.

The standard that we used in determining our bottom line was to ask ourselves what an arbitrator would give us. To my knowledge, all union professionals use this same standard. True, our guesses could sometimes be wrong, but after dealing with the same arbitrators over a period of time, we were close enough to the mark to be effective.

When we had an important grievance to process at the first, or college, level, either I or Sonia would preside over the grievance hearing. We had an understanding with the Board that if either of us, or our attorney, would be presiding, we would notify them in advance. That way, if they did not have a strong representative on that particular college campus, they could send someone more experienced from their central office.

Sometimes the college president would be the person representing management at a college-level grievance hearing. In one such instance, I and the college president exchanged pleasantries for a few minutes before I pretty much demolished his case with five cogent points. He told me afterwards that he had spent only about twenty minutes reading the case materials before the hearing, and that he would never make that mistake again. He also said, "You had five points of importance and you developed each in order with a full, but not tiresome, presentation." "Good," I replied, "and thank you kindly for noticing my efforts."

I was not really interested in winning grievances because of management's lack of knowledge or lack of preparation. Once a contract has been negotiated, it is important that both sides work in tandem to administer the contract. We wanted the other side to be as well-informed as we were about the contract and its requirements. Most of all, I wanted a system of settling problems quickly and with the preservation of our members' rights. After about eight years as President, I felt we had made a minimum of progress in that direction.

At that point, we had a large accumulation of unsettled grievances, and we approached the Board with the suggestion that we set aside one day a month to go through our list from the top down. We promised to use our best talents to hurry the process along. "Slow justice," after all, "is no justice."

I think we had more qualified people for an all-day grievance extravaganza than did the Board, so they hired Alan Drachman, an outside lawyer from Boston, to serve as their representative. In one day, we were able to settle four or five cases that had been gathering dust for some time. Alan settled in our favor very quickly on one of the cases, as it involved a clear-cut violation of the contract on the part of the Board. The entire proceeding on that one case consumed about one-and-one-half hours, compared to the seven to eight hours in hearings that had already been expended on it.

Jack Foley was not happy with this quick settlement in

our favor, and therefore was hesitant to recommend that the Board continue to use Alan's services for grievance resolution. This was ironic, as Alan had a reputation as a top-notch negotiator and a tough guy with whom to deal. Unfortunately, his efficient use of time was not in accordance with Jack's habitual delaying tactics.

In handling grievances, we sometimes had problems with our grievants, some of whom lied to us about the basis of the charges that had been brought against them. Our staff tried to make it clear to them that we would hold in the strictest confidence anything they told us, but that we expected them to tell us the truth so that we could defend them properly.

If grievants would not take our advice, we would regretfully inform them that we would not be able to represent them. Based on a contract provision that we had crafted in return for some concessions from management, grievants were also allowed to defend themselves. However, we strongly discouraged this practice, since most grievants were too emotionally involved, and had too little experience in the defense of employees, to do themselves justice. We would tell grievants who insisted on going their own way that we were opposed to their self-defense both because we thought that they would lose, and also because we did not want to see their cases added to a list of lost grievances that management could use as precedent. At this point, grievants would usually cave, and allow us to represent them. Once in a while, however, they did succeed without our help, which was not a problem.

Overall, we were not a particularly grievous lot. Our first impulse was always to try to effect a settlement, and we were prepared to settle quickly. We had plenty of other things to do than settle grievances. Since we were strong supporters of the community colleges' budget, we were heavily engaged in state and local politics. Unfortunately, management was not dominated by leaders who believed in settling things on a fair and honest basis, but they could always do business with us.

Since the first level of grievance hearings always took place at the college where the grievant was located, this produced localized training schools for union activists, a situation that helped build our strength as an organization. Bob Vater and I, and others of our ilk, wanted to motivate our members to participate more fully in their own governance. "Power is lying on the ground," I would often say to our members. "All you have to do is lean over and pick it up." We wanted to win the members to our view of how to conduct ourselves, and we used conflicts and disputes to demonstrate our ideas. If we had an opportunity to meet with a college president on a hot issue, we would turn up with one or two dozen of our members: our goal was always to produce a settlement. We did not yell or scream. We preferred a quiet, logical discussion with carefully thought-out arguments for our position. In order to get settlements, therefore, we had to be willing to compromise. Our standard for appropriate settlements was always the same: to ask ourselves what an arbitrator would give us, provided that we went that route.

One morning, I received a phone call from the president of our chapter at Norwalk Community College. The Dean of Students there considered himself an expert on style, and wanted our members to always dress according to his notion of appropriate attire. He believed, for one thing, that men should wear neckties at all times. He also thought that motorcycle boots made a bad impression on the general public, and wanted to ban their wearing by faculty members. Discussions between the Dean and our people on the value of individual expression had gone nowhere. The Norwalk chapter president asked me what they should do.

I thought about it for a minute and then said, "Go back and tell the Dean politely that you do not agree with his opinions on appropriate dress. Tell him that you have talked about this problem with your union office in Hartford, and that if he establishes his desired dress code over our objections, we will order about 100 neckties for our Norwalk members with the 4 C's distinctive logo embroidered in white against a blue background. Also inform him that, after assuring ourselves that the Norwalk female members would agree to this, we will ask them to wear these neckties, as well, not with a suit or a jacket, but over a t-shirt, a sweater, or a blouse. We will then use letters to the editor in the Norwalk newspapers to launch a public discussion of the entire issue.

The Dean of Students backed off; I do not believe that the president of Norwalk would have agreed with the Dean's plan, anyway. We therefore had a victory without any grievance whatsoever. Moreover, this kind of victory demonstrated the solidarity of our union members and their ability to be reasonable advocates for their own point of view.

Another example along these same lines involved a more substantial issue. A female teacher of Spanish, recognized as outstanding in many quarters, was, through no fault of her own, being doggedly surveilled and harassed by a student on one of our campuses. The student went so far as to frequently peer through the window of the classroom in which she taught. The teacher's requests for her college to provide her with some protection had gone unnoticed.

Her upset feelings, and our fears for her safety, prompted me to immediately call the Executive Director of the Board of Trustees, and demand some action. Again, I remained polite, and expressed my willingness to let him run the system without any interference from us. The only problem was that he was not running the system. The unyielding tone of my voice, always civil, led him to do something. I did not need, in this case, to mention our alternatives, which could have been to make a public fuss, form a student protective league to constantly accompany the teacher around the campus, and so forth. Under the circumstances, the Executive Director feared—and with good reason—that we would take some action that would prove that management had been neglectful of their lawful duties. Just two weeks earlier, at another college, a student and a teacher had had a yelling match over a grade, and the very next day the teacher's car had been broken into and trashed. The college, unaccountably, had refused to investigate this occurrence.

With regard to the Spanish teacher, the college quickly responded to pressure from the Board of Trustees' central office, and banned the stalker from the campus. What was needed was prompt action to prevent a possible tragedy, and we were able to get that without filing a grievance. We were smart, and also street-smart. Our concerns had been merited, especially because student attacks on teachers were being reported more widely in the media at that time.

As I thought later about this incident, I could not understand how the college had at first failed to act on this teacher's behalf. It was apparent that there was a serious flaw in our entire community college system. No one was watching the store, and the general attitude of management was, "If you don't criticize me, I won't criticize you." This point was proved to my own satisfaction when a personal friend of mine was named to the community colleges' Board of Trustees. She was a risk-taker, and agreed to obtain for me from their personnel files a copy of the evaluations of all of the twelve college presidents. There was not one word of criticism of any of the presidents in their evaluations, nor a single piece of advice on how to improve in any area of their work. As my grandmother, may she rest in peace, would have said, "This is by you a way to run a college?" Or to run anything, I might have added.

I put the evaluations away in a safe: fortunately, I never needed to use them for extra leverage. I was later told by an administrator who had occasion to review the work of management in the system, that in the years he was in contact with the so-called leaders and their staffs, he had never heard anyone in that group make a solid report of what went on. My dismay arose not only in defense of the rights of our members, but in the disastrous effect that such a system of unaccountability had on everyone employed at the community colleges.

I was not anti-leadership; I was for leadership by example. I tried hard to put my own leadership in that context. For instance, during the great explosion of marijuana use, I strongly wanted to participate, but I did not. I did not want to be apprehended using a banned substance and thus bring discredit upon our union. For my own inspiration, I looked to the leadership of a number of generals on D-Day during the invasion of France in World War II. Several reports by their men stated that their generals had said things such as, "If we stay here and do nothing, we will all be killed. Let's run up to the top of the hill. Some of us will get hit, but most of will make it, and we'll take care of the bastards." So they had grabbed their rifles, and shouted, "Follow me!" This was the kind of leadership by example I was talking about. In our community college system, a few top administrators would sometimes instruct us to "follow me" and then would disappear. I learned early in life that if you want to be a leader, you have to be willing to put yourself on the line.

With some noteworthy—and welcome—exceptions among management, it was mainly the teaching and professional staff who fought in defense of our rights and of the rights of our students. Our members were proud of me, and I was proud of them. Together, we demonstrated leadership by example, and courage in the face of adversity. I think that our activism served as an inspiration to the students in the community college system. Certainly, a number of students participated in our rallies and protests, knowing that our efforts could only better the education they were striving to attain. In this way, empowering the workers and helping the students went hand-in-hand.

Activists throughout the state were thus able to make the dream of a successful community college system a reality. The affordable and high-quality education we provided was a result of the efforts of people at all levels of the system. I think our greatest achievement was not the number of students whom we taught a particular subject. It was that we were able to instill a new sense of accomplishment and self-worth into hundreds—even thousands—of students, and prepare them for life and its hard knocks. The fact that we were able to do this while at the same time providing a brighter economic existence for our members meant that everybody won. Despite the many obstacles we faced, we became a force to be reckoned with in higher education in the state of Connecticut.

Sidney Lipshires holds a Ph.D. from the University of Connecticut and taught history for 30 years at Manchester Community College. He was one of the founding members of the Congress of Connecticut Community Colleges, a statewide union for teaching and professional staff, and served as its president from 1977 through 1995. He was also a founder of Connecticut's Pension Coordinating Committee and represented state employees on the Connecticut Investment Advisory Council from 1984 through 1996. His first book was *Herbert Marcuse: From Marx to Freud and Beyond* (Schenkman Publishing Company, 1974). He lives in West Hartford, Connecticut.